Lisa Aparicio, series editor

do

ENGAGING YOUTH IN DISCIPLESHIP

Jaime Román Araya • Nicholas Barasa
Milton Gay • Nabil Habiby
Andrea Sawtelle • Bakhoh Jatmiko

ISBN 978-1-63580-201-6 rev 2019-07-02

DIGITAL PRINTING

CREDITS
Authors: Kenny Wade, Jaime Román Araya, Nicholas Barasa, Milton Gay, Nabil Habiby, Andrea Sawtelle, Bakhoh Jatmiko

Book and Series Editor: Lisa Aparicio

Copy Editors: Hailey Teeter, Emily Reyes, and Emily Knocke

Cover Design: Christian Cardona

Original Content Translators: Samuel Aparicio (Chapter 1 & 3)

TABLE OF CONTENTS

ABOUT THIS SERIES

"How do you guide youth to be confident in evangelism?"

"What should I be thinking about to make sure my youth are growing in their faith?"

"Sometimes I don't feel like I know what I'm doing as a leader. How am I going to help my youth develop their own leadership skills?"

We frequently hear questions like these from youth leaders all around the world. They are youth leaders in small churches and large churches. They are formally trained youth pastors and lay volunteer youth workers. Maybe you've asked questions like these as well.

This three-book series is our way of reaching out to local youth leaders to encourage and equip you in the deeply meaningful work you are doing. The challenge is that youth ministry is diverse, with ever-changing cultural nuances to navigate. Thus, we have chosen to focus each of these books on one of our core strategies in NYI — evangelism (BE), discipleship (DO), and leadership development (GO). These core strategies have served youth ministry in the Church of the Nazarene well since its earliest days. We have also invited in a diverse team of writers to help us share a balanced perspective with you. We trust you will enjoy this blend of voices and that the mix of perspectives will provide connection to your ministry setting no matter what your context.

Wherever you find yourself in ministry, know that you are appreciated, that you are prayed for, and that you bring more skills to youth ministry than you know.

May God bless you.

Gary Hartke
Director, Nazarene Youth International

PREFACE

When we talk about evangelism (BE), discipleship (DO), and leadership development (GO), it is generally easier for us to access voices similar to our own — ones who share ideas and strategies we are already familiar with. However, we believe our three core strategies in Nazarene Youth International deserve a more nuanced discussion. We started this conversation in 2013 with a renewed emphasis on our core strategies and started talking about BE, DO, and GO.

Evangelism:
BE God's light, even in the dark places of our world.

Discipleship:
DO the hard work of becoming more like Jesus as you walk with others.

Leadership Development:
GO out into your community and learn as a servant leader.

As the conversation of BE, DO, and GO spread, we wanted to help the lessons emerging from those conversations to spread as well. We wanted the lessons to be taught by diverse voices, each bringing a unique perspective to the global conversation. To accomplish this, we needed a global team of writers, and the result was this series, which we believe is a true expression of what it means to be a global church.

We trust that you will benefit greatly from these diverse authors. A brief introduction for each one is provided at the beginning of their chapter. As you read, you will be reminded of the diversity of our church, not only through the content, but even in little ways, such as spelling. We have made the intentional choice to keep the vocabulary and spelling style for each author consistent with what is used in their part of the world. When a chapter has been translated from a different language, the spelling and vocabulary are more reflective of the translator's home country.

May God bless you in your ministry as you seek to actively engage your youth in evangelism, discipleship, and leadership development. We believe these books are starting points to help you move forward in your ministry with more intentionality. Where will you go from here? We invite you to take your place in the global story of BE, DO, and GO.

Lisa Aparicio
Editor
Ministry Development Coordinator, Nazarene Youth International

ACKNOWLEDGMENTS

The formation of a global writing team required the input and support of many individuals. It began with an invitation for all of our regional youth coordinators to share names with us of youth leaders from their region who excelled in evangelism, discipleship, or leadership development. Without the support and discernment of Ronald Miller (Africa Region), Janary Suyat de Godoy (Asia-Pacific Region), Diego Lopez (Eurasia Region), Milton Gay (Mesoamerica Region), Jimmy De Gouveia (South America Region), and Justin Pickard (USA/Canada Region) these books wouldn't have happened.

Video conference calls were hosted with all of the 18 writers to share, collaborate, and ultimately shape the structure of these books. The calls were organized and led by Shannon Greene (Global NYI Office). Her overall contribution to this project was absolutely invaluable. Kenny Wade (Youth in Mission) also participated in each call to share the background of the BE, DO, GO initiative. The context he provided gave the whole project a solid foundation to build on. Kenny also contributed to the series as the author of the introductions.

Ultimately though, these books wouldn't have been possible without the hard work of each of our writers. They have shared from their hearts about how they see God at work through the church's efforts to engage youth in evangelism, discipleship, and leadership development.

Africa
Wesley Parry (Evangelism)
Nicholas Barasa (Discipleship)
Lesego Shibambo
(Leadership Development)

Asia-Pacific
Daniel Latu (Evangelism)
Bakhoh Jatmiko (Discipleship)
Cameron Batkin
(Leadership Development)

Eurasia
Wouter van der Zeijden (Evangelism)
Nabil Habiby (Discipleship)
Kat Wood (Leadership Development)

Mesoamerica
Dario Richards (Evangelism)
Milton Gay (Discipleship)
Odily Díaz (Leadership Development)

South America
Christiano Malta (Evangelism)
Jaime Román Araya (Discipleship)
Thiago Nieman Ambrósio
(Leadership Development)

USA/Canada
Denise Holland (Evangelism)
Andrea Sawtelle (Discipleship)
Phil Starr (Leadership Development)

INTRODUCTION

Kenny Wade

Kenny Wade serves as the Youth in Mission Coordinator. Kenny believes youth ministry helps us think creatively about what it means for God's kingdom to come here on earth as we minister alongside youth whose lives are committed to Christ. He believes that discipleship is a life-giving, corrective, and formative cycle of being the church.

The DO of discipleship flows from the BE of living in relationship with Christ. Discipleship is the mission of joining God in the work He is doing in the world (Matthew 28:18-20). Discipleship is about allowing our lives to be formed in the process of following Jesus. With our whole person, we journey in community — engaging in God's mission that is already present while inviting others to do the same. A missionary who served among the aboriginal people of Northwest Australia for over 20 years told me that their method of discipleship is loving God, loving others, and teaching others to do the same (Luke 10:27). Sounds familiar, right? Discipleship is our central calling and mission as Good News people. It's what we DO.

My friend Bobby (that I began sharing about in the introduction for the BE book) taught me heaps about discipleship. Jesus' Spirit was already alive and active and drawing Bobby to Him. I didn't want to get in the way or mess things up! It's as though I was being trusted with Bobby and God was preparing both of us for the journey ahead. God was using me to nurture him into a deeper sense of identity of faith in Christ. However, God was also teaching me through Bobby to be content simply traveling alongside someone at their own pace, waiting to notice how God was at work. We were both being discipled.

> **Discipleship means taking action in ways that align with what we believe.**

Leonard Sweet sees evangelism and discipleship on the same continuum of growth in God's grace.[1] Evangelism can be viewed as the initial stages of disciple-making. Discipleship is about learning and growing in grace, both for us and others. Discipleship means taking action in ways that align with what we believe. We DO things that help us grow. We DO things that help others grow. Discipleship is the action of doing that flows from the being with Christ.

Being in Christ results in the DO of sharing Good News through our lives. Our example is the life of Jesus and His mission (Luke 4). We follow in the footsteps of our master by contextualizing the Good News and living out timeless examples of Christ-centered living. Prayer. Scripture. Solitude. Community. Worship. Sacrifice. Compassion. Learning. Serving. Discipleship begins out of a personal relationship with God and pours over into all other relationships. Discipleship does not happen on its own. Discipleship is best when practiced in tension — the tension of being a disciple of Jesus by drawing close to God. Practicing what Jesus did in being the Good News, then inviting others to do the same. We must be discipled by someone and be discipling someone else. Sometimes we are discipled by those older than we are; other times by those younger than we are. Age and longevity of faith in Christ are important, but not as important as the dynamics of a teachable spirit. As a lifelong learner, I may be selective in who I allow to instruct and influence my discipleship journey; when I practice a teachable spirit, anyone of any age and background can become channels of God's grace to shape and form my faith in Christ. We can only share, mentor, and lead in the ways we have experienced and chosen to grow.

Discipleship is not a solitary experience. We cannot grow in relationship with Christ unless we are growing in relationship with others.

Bobby wanted to grow but didn't know how to. He wanted to believe, but he was not sure he could. He needed someone to journey alongside him in this quest. He needed the faith community of the church. More importantly for the early conversations, he needed a member of the Body of Christ just to be a friend and love him for who he was as a fellow image bearer of God. Bobby needed Christian community to discover trust in Christ just as much as I needed friendship outside the relationships of the church to authentically engage in the mission of God.

The conversation in the doorway of his home and his question about church had led to the coffee shop and back onto the athletic field as we coached together. Now, Bobby was asking about church again. Our discipling friendship was moving toward a greater vision of community in the Body of Christ. Discipleship is not a solitary experience. We cannot grow in relationship with Christ unless we are growing in relationship with others (Mark 12:30-31). Likewise, we cannot truly grow in relationship with others unless we are growing in relationship with Christ. The dynamics of these relationships are where we practice and how we experience the holiness of living and being transformed into the image of Christ. Discipleship is growing in our love of God and love of others and then teaching others to do the same. Discipleship is something we DO and something we allow to BE done to us.

Healthy discipleship is being a disciple of Christ while being discipled and discipling others. We share with others how we are growing so that they can learn to experience how to go deeper in Christ and grow in reflection of the restored image of God. In some ways, the relationship of discipleship mirrors that of a parent and child. Like it or not, our parents, if they are our primary caregivers, have the greatest influence on us as children. Our lives mirror the time we have spent with them (and away from them). Our lives echo the patterns they have set and the ruts they have cut with their decisions, habits, and experiences. If you are a parent, then your own children are a relational priority of Christ-centered discipleship (1 Timothy 3:12). Christ-following parents have primary discipling responsibility for their children.

These close relationships are often the most difficult to BE and DO in following Christ. This challenge makes them the most important relationships in which to strive for growth, grace, and reflection of the love and patience of Christ. If we tend to these relationships to the best of our ability in Christ, then all the other areas of discipleship will follow. Our own children can be our greatest teachers.[2] Choosing to have a teachable spirit in the relationships where we are most vulnerable is an important foundation for a developing disciple.

All the coffee, coaching, and church conversations with Bobby were cultivating a discipleship friendship between us with Christ as our guide. Bobby had expressed to me the yearning he had for peace, joy, and freedom. He had witnessed me experiencing these relational side effects of faith in Christ through my doubts, fears, decisions, and frustrations in the journey together (1 Corinthians 11:1). Often, I would remind him that those faith realities were only possible because of a relational trust in Christ.

What do I have to offer to the community of faith without a deepening relationship with Christ?

During one of our early coffee conversations, he had inquired into the details of my process for trusting God with decisions in life. I shared with him a discernment practice I had adopted from interpreting Scripture — the practice of holding faith and life in the tension of reason (common sense), experience (in my life and others), Scripture (God's story), and tradition (Christian community through history to the present day).[3] Bobby condensed my explanation into a simple acronym: "R-E-S-T." Lost to his meaning I asked, "What do you mean?" He reiterated, "Reason, Experience, Scripture, and Tradition. That makes sense. We can BE at rest in God with our decisions." Pretty sure I had a "God-moment" there, with Bobby teaching me about what I claimed to practice in discerning the decisions of life. Again, I was being discipled.

What do I have to offer to the community of faith without a deepening relationship with Christ? How can I truly discover who I am within the image of God unless I am committed to the nurturing and fellowship of others? Discipleship is both an individual and collective effort. Discipleship leads into the community of faith and sends into the context of culture. I cannot be a Christ-follower without others to sharpen, gauge, and balance my journey of faith with diversity in life and experience. We must BE in Christ, so we can DO what He did with and for others. Disciples. Let's make those. Let's DO that.

CHAPTER 1

Biblical Foundations of Discipleship

Jaime Román Araya

Jaime Román Araya is the Field Youth Coordinator in Chile and a pastor who serves in Santiago de Chile. Youth ministry is exciting to him because he gets the opportunity to present the gospel in its fullness, in the language of the new generation. He sees discipleship as important because without maturity, there is no growth. For Jaime, discipleship means investing your life in the lives of others.

"Hello friends, it's nice to meet you! I am a young pastor and am responsible for a discipleship strategy that involves a large number of people. However, for this task I have decided to concentrate my efforts on working primarily with a specific group of men and women. I'm actually coming to the end of my current ministry assignment, so lately I've been focused on preparing this group to disciple others. We do not have an easy path ahead. We will certainly face hard times along the way and this will cause many to doubt our work together. Nonetheless, I am determined to accompany them in this adventure as long as I can. I know they are going to change the world. Maybe you find yourself in a situation similar to mine. I invite you to follow my example and share your experience with others who need to learn from you. By the way, I think I forgot to introduce myself. My name is Jesus and I'm from Nazareth."

Almost 20 centuries ago, this young man of approximately thirty years of age began His ministry among ordinary men and women like you and me. He took His work so seriously that the message He entrusted to this fledgling group of believers has survived innumerable wars, calamities, constant antagonism, and brutal persecution. The miraculous survival of the gospel means that we can continue fulfilling the same Great Commission given to those first disciples.

On occasion, Jesus' physical fatigue was apparent enough for everyone to notice as He faced situations which tested His patience. After ministering to multitudes of people who brought their needs to Him, Jesus fell asleep and rested in a fragile wooden boat while He and His disciples crossed to the other side of the Sea of Galilee. Despite being overtaken by a powerful storm, Jesus slept on. As the storm continued, the disciples could no longer contain their fear and so they woke Jesus up, knowing their lives were in danger. It is here that Jesus calls out his disciples, saying, "You of little faith, why are you so afraid?" (Matthew 8:26). The disciples were just learning who Jesus was, and yet their slowness to believe is evidence of the patience Jesus had with them as He walked with them on their journeys of faith. We would have had the same reaction as Jesus, or likely worse, if someone unexpectedly interrupted our rest after a long day of hard work. This was Jesus, a young pastor who lived out the ministry entrusted to Him by His Father, enduring (and also enjoying) on a daily basis the humanity of the imperfect disciples He Himself had chosen.

In Jesus we find the perfect model of a pastor's heart, full of love and grace, which was masterfully described by King David almost 1,000 years before the birth of the Messiah:

> "You, my God, are my shepherd; I lack nothing with you.
> You make me rest in green pastures,
> and to calm my thirst you take me to calm waters.
> You give me new strength and guide me in the best way,
> because that's the way you are.
> I can cross dangerous places and not be afraid of anything,
> because you are my pastor and you are always by my side;
> you guide me on the right path and fill me with confidence.
> Even if my enemies get angry, you offer me a banquet
> and you fill me with happiness; You give me special treatment!
> I am completely sure that your kindness and your love
> they will accompany me while I live,
> and that I will live forever where you live." (Psalm 23, CEB)

With a pastor's heart and while knowing the imperfect nature of His team, Jesus discipled them by sharing principles and truths with methods that left a mark on their lives and on the lives of those around them. The Master shared His teachings in daily life, without organizing conferences, seminars, or conventions — even when doctrinal or foundational issues arose. Jesus was practical and simple in implementing His methodology. For example, we see Him spitting on the earth to make mud and heal a man blind from birth and riding a donkey in His triumphal entrance into Jerusalem. Whenever there was an opportunity to adapt simple elements from His surroundings to illustrate a teaching, Jesus did not waste time to take advantage of the chance to instruct his followers.

We see in the Bible how Jesus formed His disciples in the streets, walking long hours and days in the sun, going hungry, being cold and tired. The Lord shared His life with rabbis and prostitutes, with Roman officials and hopeless paralytics. He had no problem sitting at the table with tax collectors and other infamous sinners. His mission was clear to Him, and He wasted no time trying to follow the social and religious traditions imposed by men. Rather, He invested all of His resources in taking care of His flock.

After going on long journeys to preach, heal the sick, and work miracles, the Master preferred to eat a good sandwich (hot dog, arepa, or whatever your country's most popular sandwich is) with His friends in a local shop than to retire to a luxurious room in some inn to rest alone. By opening His daily life to them, Jesus transmitted the most important message of the universe to His disciples. These imperfect followers who did not yet grasp the glorious mission they were about to receive — even after sharing life with the very Son of God — these disciples were transformed through their daily interactions with Jesus.

Because of the clarity with which Jesus presents His strategy to us through the Scriptures, we see that discipleship is more of a life process than an activity or department within our church. Dr. Lucas Leys writes, "Discipleship … begins the moment we enter into the membership of the body (the church) and it will end in heaven." He adds, "Being disciples and friends of Christ means that we want to live as He taught us. Discipleship is not a program or just a method. Discipleship means practicing the disciplines of Christ to such an extent that our lives might spread the same kind of obedience to others. We must live out Christ's teachings in order to 'teach' them to our young people."[2]

Just about anyone can pass on information about the Christian faith. To do that you just need a pencil and a booklet where you fill in biblical verses. However, in order to transmit life principles, you need to deeply love God and have a willingness to allow yourself to be shaped by the hands of the Master Potter.

In our youth ministries, we need to make sure that we are not being lax in the work we are doing with new believers. Too often we respond to the need to disciple young believers by offering a few lessons of a Bible class to teach the "biblical foundations of Christianity." We act as if we expect our youth to "graduate" as a disciple of Jesus at the end of the classes, as if they were a university graduate. Unfortunately, as soon as the ceremony ends and the lights, applause, and congratulations disappear, we usually abandon them to their fate, hoping this "new disciple" will make the decision to be baptized, so that in the short term, he or she will be received as a member of the church. We might even hope that one day they will hear the voice of God calling them into ministry so we might see the fruits of our efforts.

This rudimentary system has been used by many, but it bears no resemblance to the discipleship models we see in the Bible. It is time for us to evaluate our discipleship strategies and make whatever changes are necessary in order to align ourselves to the model Christ gave us: a model which recognizes and responds to the true importance of discipleship for new believers. Our youth are looking to us to help them build a strong foundation required for the Christian life. More importantly, God expects us to make true and faithful disciples, not just "converts." It is time we take on this responsibility!

Our Task

The Great Commission, along with extending the challenge to leave everything behind in order to announce the gospel message, also called the believers to help new believers learn and be shaped by the teachings and commands of Jesus. Accepting the call to "GO" is foundational, but we must not forget that it is only the first part of the Great Commission. The work of strengthening, discipling, and forming followers of Christ is the second part many of us leave undone. So, what does Jesus mean when He commands us to make disciples?

We are concerned about doing the work of God, but are we intentionally preparing the next generation to boldly live out their faith in order to carry on the most important message in the universe?

To disciple, in simple words, is to transmit to others the message we have received and to make sure that they fulfill the same mission with the same passion. The great apostle Paul understood this idea of discipleship very well, as he shared with his young disciple Timothy: "You have heard me teach things that have been confirmed by many reliable witnesses. Now teach these truths to other trustworthy people who will be able to pass them on to others" (2 Timothy 2:2, NLT). In short, Paul was saying, "Tim, make sure this message does not die with you!"

We must be honest with ourselves and assess our own ministries. We are concerned about doing the work of God, but are we intentionally preparing the next generation to boldly live out their faith in order to carry on the most important message in the universe?

In order to fulfill the mission of making disciples, we must also allow others to advise, guide, and disciple us. In ministry, it is essential for us to look for mentors, people with maturity, experience, and spiritual authority who we can be accountable to, ask for advice, be corrected by. Felix Ortiz describes a mentor in this way:

> "A mentor is neither a father, nor a partner, nor God, nor someone perfect; he or she is simply a Christian who is firmly committed to grow in their knowledge of Jesus, to accept Him as Lord and Savior, to follow Him and to help other believers to deepen their own experience with the Lord. From this, two important truths are inferred: 1) A mentor is an active follower of Jesus, 2) who helps other believers to be active followers of Jesus."[3]

It is healthy and necessary to be moldable and recognize how much we need correction from someone else, especially when we are promoted to increasingly higher levels of leadership. We must never forget we are also sheep following the Good Shepherd. As Francisco Cifuentes, a Chilean pastor, expresses it, "I am a sheep that stands on two legs on Sunday."

If we are not conformed to Christ, we will be forming personal disciples after our own hearts, disciples who follow our example and make decisions based on our humanity and not on the image of Jesus we should be reflecting.

If Jesus Himself went to the Father every day, in intimacy and humility, how much more must we! Today, ask God for a teachable heart and spirit.

It is ethically and practically impossible to form young people according to the heart of God if we do not know the heart of God ourselves. To get to know someone, at any level, we must spend time with them. Consequently, an intimate and continuous relationship with God enables you naturally and supernaturally to fulfill the great task of forming disciples of Christ. If we are not conformed to Christ, we will be forming personal disciples after our own hearts, disciples who follow our example and make decisions based on our humanity and not on the image of Jesus we should be reflecting. We should regularly ask ourselves this question: Am I forming disciples of my own or disciples of Jesus?

There is a popular saying which goes, "the lazy person works double." I believe this phrase conveys very well the tremendous burden which results from trying to disciple others even when we have become spiritually lazy, forgetting to spend time daily in spiritual habits for our own personal growth. On the other hand, when we spend time with God in a disciplined way, those around us are being discipled by our example and character that is increasingly becoming more like Jesus. This was the goal Paul entrusted to the Ephesians: "This will continue until we all come to such unity in our faith and knowledge of God's Son that we will be mature in the Lord, measuring up to the full and complete standard of Christ" (Ephesians 4:13, NLT).

The question at hand then is: How did Jesus disciple others?

Although He did it informally and without leaving us a step-by-step instruction manual, when we read the Gospels we can see how Jesus' discipleship strategy falls into four areas of influence. These can be classified by the size of the audience He was working with. With much wisdom, the Teacher allocated resources and invested time according to what each group needed to achieve different levels of impact, trust, and intimacy.

Thus, we are going to look at the ways Jesus uniquely carried out discipleship with the crowds, the larger group of followers (known as "the 72"), the twelve apostles, and finally, the small intimate group of three disciples. We will study each group a little and Jesus' level of influence on them.

The Crowds

Jesus begins His public ministry in a big crowd as He is baptized and recognized as the Messiah by His cousin John the Baptist in the Jordan River. Although it was not His priority, Jesus dedicated part of His time to sharing His life, teachings, and service with large groups of people which sometimes numbered in the thousands.

The best-known accounts of His discipleship work with groups this size are the "Sermon on the Mount" (Gospel of Matthew, chapter 5) and the "Feeding of the Five Thousand" (Gospel of John, chapter 6).

With this size of audience, Jesus limited Himself to sharing general teachings which could be applied to any person and any situation, and He invested His time in performing miracles according to the needs that arose. There was no possible way for Jesus to do personal, in-depth work with each individual He encountered, yet, He demonstrated His care and concern for the crowds by ministering to their needs.

Perhaps this is the most common way to disciple, using the traditional church approach. The pastor, leader, or teacher is limited to guiding his or her group from behind a pulpit, thus using preaching to correct and instruct the congregation. The advantage of this approach is that a large number of people can be influenced at the same time, but a disadvantage is the inability to attend to each person's unique needs and questions.

Crowds or congregations as areas of influence provide good opportunities to do large-scale discipleship. However, it cannot be the only way we engage people in discipleship.

The Large Group

Only the Gospel of Luke (chapter 10) contains the time when Jesus commissioned a group of 72 disciples (or 70, depending on the version of the Bible you use) to fulfill the task of visiting the cities where he planned to go later. The disciples divided up in pairs to preach and perform healings among the people.

To form a group of 72 people, Jesus had to choose some people from among the crowds who followed Him and set them apart in order to ask a higher level of commitment from them. This would indicate that Jesus probably spent more time with the 72 than with the crowds. He invested His life and teachings into them in a greater capacity than with the crowds.

Into this category we can also include the group of believers who remained united and persevered after the ascension of Christ, a group mentioned in chapter 1 of the book of the Acts. Among all those who belonged to this group, Matthias was chosen as the apostle who would be Judas Iscariot's successor. The requirements were for this person to have followed Jesus throughout His time on earth and to have witnessed His Resurrection. With this passage, we are reminded of the group of faithful men and women who followed Jesus from the beginning of His ministry here on earth and who responded with a greater commitment to the discipleship they received from Christ. Thus, Jesus was able to invest in and disciple them more intensely.

It is necessary to pay attention to those people in your ministry who are showing signs of growth in their commitment and relationship with Jesus and who also show interest in service inside and outside the church. Just like Jesus did, we should begin to entrust those who are getting closer to

God with some responsibilities, as they will be establishing their place in the Body and using their gifts for the Kingdom.

The Small Group

In reading the Gospels, the amount of time Jesus invested in one specific group of followers, the twelve apostles, really stands out. Except for His times of prayer and personal retreats, Jesus spent most of His days with these twelve disciples. He lived the last three years of His life on Earth with this select group of men, sharing every situation life presented them, no matter how common. He took advantage of the trust, transparency, and closeness provided by such a small group of people to train the apostles and to show them the lifestyle He expected of them.

Clearly, working with small groups is not about a church growth system or a passing fad used in contemporary church ministries. Jesus Himself teaches us that the greatest fruit of His ministry did not come out of the time spent with the multitudes but by investing quality time with His closest disciples. It is in this context where Jesus was able to produce a powerful, authentic, and eternal impact on the life of each apostle.

Whether you call them small groups, cells groups, seeds, houses of prayer, life groups, connection groups, centers of blessing, friendship groups, or the most original name you can think of, you must make it a priority for you and your other youth leaders to spend time pouring your life into your youth. It is critical to share life with our youth and help them see their own responsibility for and role in fulfilling the Great Commission.

I encourage you to organize your time so that you can spend a couple of hours each week going out with your small group for coffee or ice cream and talk about what it means to live in holiness and enjoy life in God. These are the moments your youth will never forget and will likely replicate with those whom they are discipling.

Relationships in ministry do not happen automatically but must be intentionally constructed. Dr. Lucas Leys writes:

> "Effective leaders know that students do not need preachers, theologians, or therapists as much as mature friends who know how to model the Christian life and can share that life with them. Relational ministry

is about helping young people to maturity and purpose through friendship and relational work."[4]

These small groups are critical because the limited time available to us during the youth group gathering is not enough to convey all the biblical principles and truths of life that our youth need in order to survive in this increasingly confusing and secular society. The enemy wants to keep us separated, because he knows that we are stronger together. Take the initiative of Jesus and invest your life in the youth God has entrusted to you. The Christian life was designed to be enjoyed in community, not in solitude.

The Intimate Group

The apostle Paul declared, "God does not show favoritism" (Romans 2:11). However, Jesus certainly had disciples (and friends) with whom He shared some of the most unique and important moments in His ministry.

In studying the story of Jesus resurrecting the daughter of Jairus in the gospel of Mark, chapter 5, verses 37 and 40 state that Jesus allowed only three of His disciples to accompany Him to the house and enter with Him to the room where the little girl was. They were Peter, James, and John.

If you jump to chapter 9 of the same book and stop in verse 2, you will see Jesus is once again accompanied by the same three disciples: Peter, James, and John. On that occasion, something so supernatural and shocking happens that it causes the disciples to tremble with fear, and they could not contain their astonishment. Verse 10 provides an interesting detail — they kept this event a secret. This attitude clearly highlights the trust that existed between the Rabbi and his three closest disciples.

We also see the significance of this close connection in the final moments before the crucifixion as Jesus invites the same three apostles to stay closest to Him:

> "He took Peter and the two sons of Zebedee along with him, and he began to be sorrowful and troubled. Then he said to them, 'My soul is overwhelmed with sorrow to the point of death. Stay here and keep watch with me.' Going a little farther, he fell with his face to the ground and prayed, 'My Father, if it is possible, may this cup be taken from me. Yet not as I will, but as you will.'" (Mathew 26:37-39)

The unique feature of this intimate sphere of influence is how Jesus shared the most difficult moment of His ministry with only His three most trusted disciples, Peter, James, and John. This teaches us how important it is for the youth whom we are discipling to be participants not only in the happy moments we enjoy in life but in the difficult moments as well. It is necessary for them to see us as human beings who are vulnerable to pain and need, to see real flesh and blood leaders who depend on the Father in all circumstances of life. They need to see this in us in order to know that their own fears, doubts, and struggles do not disqualify them from walking with Jesus. It is reassuring to know that there is no such thing as a perfect, self-sufficient, or untouchable leader.

Our Discipleship Groups

Seeing and understanding the discipleship styles Jesus used in His discipleship should challenge and motivate us to make sure we are intentionally engaging these groups in discipleship. Discipleship must always be seen as something more than just transmitting information to memorize. Jesus poured out His life on all those around Him, even while His influence was always intensified on those closest to Him.

In his book, *The 21 Irrefutable Laws of Leadership*, John Maxwell calls the last of his laws for effective leaders "The Law of Legacy," which states that, "A leader's lasting value is measured by succession."[5] Maxwell writes:

> "Almost anyone can make an organization look good for a moment — launching a new show or striking product, attracting crowds to a large activity, or radically reducing the budget to reinforce the fundamentals. But leaders who leave a legacy take different measures. They lead with both today and tomorrow in mind."[6]

Discipleship must always be seen as something more than just transmitting information to memorize.

This thought could also be applied to discipleship and is seen in Jesus and what and how He taught. The Messiah had all the authority and power to respond to the constant request of His disciples to free Israel from the Roman Empire, organizing a great revolt with catastrophic consequences and in the end, get all the credit for the victory. However, the wise Teacher of Galilee, with humility and modesty, with love and respect for the Father, invested His ministry in the complex task of forming disciples and leaders who could succeed Him when He was no longer there.

As you read the remaining chapters of this book and explore new or different ways to engage youth in discipleship, seek to follow the example of Jesus. Take seriously the work of passing the good news. Leave a legacy. Paul's advice to Titus, a youth pastor: "In the same way, encourage the young men to live wisely. And you yourself must be an example to them by doing good works of every kind. Let everything you do reflect the integrity and seriousness of your teaching" (Titus 2:6-7, NLT).

CHAPTER 2

As You Begin: Disciples Making Disciples

Nicholas Barasa

Nicholas Barasa is the East Africa Field Youth Coordinator who serves in Nairobi, Kenya. Youth ministry is exciting to him because he loves developing leaders and impacting youth with the Word of God. Nicholas sees discipleship as the path of growth in Christlikeness. His desire is to know God and make Him known to the rest of his generation.

The church in the 21st century seems to be at a point of decision. We need to reflect critically on how we have been fulfilling, or failing at, Jesus' charge in the Great Commission to make disciples. We need to be honest with ourselves regarding the ways we are failing, repent, and change course. In Africa, it is said that Christianity is a mile wide, but an inch deep. This is a sad commentary on the Christian life in Africa, and it could be said of Christianity in many other parts of the world as well. The gospel has spread, and while people are religious, many are not truly rooted in Christ. While they say they are Christians, the heart of Christ is not reflected in their conduct and beliefs, and the seed for this duality is a lack of genuine discipleship.

Discipleship is a journey which ought to begin once a person gives his or her life to Christ. The new believer begins learning and living out the foundations of the Christian faith with the goal of discipleship being to help them grow and mature spiritually in Christ. In other words, the journey to become Christlike begins when the person surrenders all of themselves to God, and the journey continues as they surrender themselves daily. The life of Christ was blameless, and it should be the desire of every Christian to live a life that exemplifies the life of Christ.

Intentional discipleship is the key to shaping a person's life according to the values, teachings, and example of Christ.

However, discipleship cannot happen by chance. Intentional discipleship is the key to shaping a person's life according to the values, teachings, and example of Christ. Jesus chose the Twelve whom He spent all of His time with, teaching them and allowing them to learn and ask questions. For three years, Jesus walked with the Twelve so that He could send them out into the world to teach others. Our responsibility in youth ministry does not end when our youth age out of the youth group. Our responsibility is to disciple them so that by the time "we send them out into the world," they have deep roots of faith, a close relationship with God, and are ready to teach others. In order to do this, our thoughts, strategies, and resources need to be channelled towards the ministry of discipleship.

We can learn a lot from the traditional African way in which the elders would share the history and virtues to the young people orally. This ensured their youth would be able to carry on the traditions and value systems of the society as they grew up. Every opportunity the elders had to speak to the youth, they would use it to emphasize the belief system of the community. The most appropriate time to share was during the rite of passage stage. These practices show how strategic the elders were in making sure the beliefs, values, and traditions of the community did not get lost along the way. Their faithfulness to this work is how the identity of the community was passed from one generation to the next.

So, as we begin to intentionally engage our youth in discipleship, we must honestly ask ourselves whether or not we have learned the beliefs, values, and traditions of the greater Christian community. Have we embraced and are we living out the key teachings we will need to pass on to the next generation? Have we given time to our own discipleship? Are there people or groups who hold us accountable and help us along in our own journey of faith? This is key, because in life we cannot give what we don't have.

Who Is Discipling You?

While many people feel disqualified from discipling others, because they have not been intentionally discipled themselves, this does not give us permission to excuse ourselves from the Great Commission. Begin praying now for God to guide you to someone who can disciple you. Also, discipleship doesn't always look like someone older than you sitting across from you and asking questions. While that is one model, discipleship can also look like two friends who meet regularly to talk about their faith, ask hard questions, and hold each other accountable. The important thing is that we have someone who is present in our life and who will speak their heart to us, mentor, rebuke, correct, and encourage us.

To get an idea of what this can look like, we are going to reflect on three different discipling relationships throughout the Bible. These should serve both as inspiration for our own discipleship and also for the ways we think about providing discipleship for our youth.

Jethro and Moses

A unique discipling relationship which speaks to me is the relationship between Moses and his father-in-law, Jethro. Moses was a great leader who had a huge mandate to lead the nation of Israel from slavery in Egypt to the land of promise, which God had given to their forefathers. With the responsibility of leading the Israelites and serving as their intercessor before God and settling their disputes, Moses was quickly overwhelmed by the needs of the people. Moses' father-in-law noticed this and spoke to him as an advisor. From his outside perspective, Jethro saw the situation differently and was able to give Moses advice. Jethro called Moses back to his primary task, which was to "be the people's representative before God" (Exodus 18:19). Jethro also gave Moses a different model for how to lead and delegate leadership responsibilities to others.

Jethro is only mentioned twice prior to this story and doesn't appear in the biblical text after it. However, Jethro spoke words of wisdom to Moses which transformed the way Moses led and ministered. As far as we know from the text, Jethro didn't disciple Moses in an ongoing way, however, as his father-in-law, there was clearly a trusted relationship there that allowed Moses to receive the correction Jethro shared.

As a leader in the local church and in the district's youth ministry, I have had to speak into many issues; I seek out individuals who will keep me accountable, especially during those times of discernment or counsel. I know it is important to have someone holding me accountable regarding my spiritual walk and leadership. It has to be someone I trust and someone who is willing to speak honestly with me when things don't work out. As a spiritual authority in our lives, we need to consider drawing near to our pastors for this kind of discipleship and advice. As a spiritual parent, he or she is in a position to pray with us and at the same time challenge us as we grow in our relationship with God.

Therefore, pay attention. Who might God be using to speak into your life, even if it is not someone you meet with regularly? Who might God be asking you to speak with and share a truth that will help them along in their spiritual journey?

Paul and Barnabas

As Paul travelled, planting churches all over and preaching the good news of Jesus to the Gentiles, he partnered with and was accompanied by other leaders in the church. One of the key ministry partners for Paul was Barnabas. In Acts 11 we read about Barnabas and Paul beginning to do ministry together, and in Acts 13:2 the believers in Antioch are instructed by the Holy Spirit: "Set apart for me Barnabas and Saul for the work to which I have called them." The reason for this pairing is not spelled out in the text, but as the story of the early church unfolds, the need for these two leaders to have the support of the other is obvious.

As a leader in the ministry to which God has called me, I have learned the importance of having a "Barnabas" in my life. A "Barnabas" in this case is our ministry colleague or colleagues who support us in our ministry. These are people who might serve in a similar role as you, either in your own ministry or at a different church, but it should be someone you are close to, who understands what God has called you to, and is passionate about what you do. These colleagues will be there to pray with you, challenge you to become a better person, and encourage you in the journey towards being Christlike.

Youth ministry can bring a number of unique challenges and potential pitfalls across our ministry path. Walking the discipleship journey with a colleague provides us with the added benefit of having someone who understands those unique challenges and who can hold us accountable. They will know to ask you about your own spiritual journey and your relationship with God and not just about your ministry and the work you are doing in the church. They will be attentive to the decisions you are making both in and outside the church and will speak up if they have concerns.

Another strength of this kind of discipleship relationship is that you are able to provide the same kind of support and accountability for this ministry colleague. You will be cheering each other on and lifting each other up when you fall. You will be able to learn from each other, study the Bible together, and push each other to keep your relationship with God as a central priority in your lives.

Paul and Timothy

As the Holy Spirit moved Paul on from the churches he planted, Paul made sure to have leaders who carried on the ministry in each place. Other partners in the ministry would travel between the churches, carrying messages back and forth and encouraging the believers. One particular person Paul invested a lot of time in mentoring and discipling was Timothy. Timothy was a young man with a lot of energy who was passionate about ministry. We first meet Timothy in Acts as he travels often with Paul and Silas. Later in Paul's letters to various churches, he mentions Timothy and we see how Timothy is considered a co-worker and a fellow minister of the good news of Jesus. In the books 1 and 2 Timothy, we get to read the wise counsel Paul gave to Timothy. It was Paul's desire to have well discipled leaders who could carry on the ministry among these groups of young believers.

The discipleship model seen in Paul and Timothy more closely reflects what we traditionally think of when we think about discipleship. As we begin the book on engaging youth in discipleship, I've wanted to make sure we pause and consider our own discipleship and make sure that we have people encouraging us in our own walk with God. However, as Christians, we always have a responsibility to others. Our own discipleship journey must have in mind the "Timothy" in our life. Who are you investing your life in so that the next generation can grow deep roots of faith?

Natural Ways of Discipleship

There are several ways we can be engaged in disciple making in the ministry context. What works best for me in my area of ministry is to have steps of growth to allow someone to look back and see the development and growth of a new believer. This helps the disciple and the one who is discipling to assess whether or not there is progress in their journey of faith. Even with these steps, it is important to remember that discipleship is a journey and not a formula. Discipleship is all about building a lasting relationship, and therefore it is a journey both parties must be willing to walk through together. When both parties are committed to staying on this journey, it will be an enjoyable experience.

The shift from receiver to giver is a crucial step in giving a disciple room to continue their growth.

The discipleship journey can take on many forms. You can even develop a process of your own, as long as it bears fruit. The steps of "watch me," "do together," and "do as I watch" are common principles for helping people learn new skills. Here is how I use these three steps when engaging in discipleship at any level. These three steps can serve as a good way to assess the progress within any discipleship strategy.

Watch me

As a youth leader or worker, it is important to be a living example to the people you are discipling. These new believers are watching and will eventually capture the same attitude and spirit in you.

Discipleship should begin with letting the new believer see how you live out your faith. The way you practise spiritual disciplines will be a learning experience for the new convert and those young Christians. As earlier stated, it is difficult to offer what you don't have or to tell someone to do something you know very well you can't do. Therefore, let the students and youth learn from you through your lifestyle.

Just as a small baby will watch and emulate what the adults around them do in order to learn, young believers are watching us, and our choices and actions matter.

Do together

Discipleship is a journey which requires the active engagement of both parties. Encourage your young disciples to start practicing the spiritual disciplines. Let your students participate as they walk alongside you in this journey. As they read the Bible, spend time reading with them, teaching them how to pray and engage with them in fasting. Start slowly and help them incorporate these disciplines into their lives step-by-step. Whatever you are doing, let the ones you are discipling tag along with you because they are learning through "hands-on" experience.

For new believers, it is important to respect the newness of their faith and to start with "baby steps." As they grow in their faith and continue gaining confidence and strength, you can expect more of them.

Do as I watch

Eventually, as you begin to see your disciple maturing in their faith and living out what they believe more and more, you can give them responsibilities such as leading small group devotions, leading in prayer, engaging in evangelism, and taking up other ministry responsibilities. Inviting them to lead is not just a leadership development task but a disciple-shaping one as well. The shift from receiver to giver is a crucial step in giving a disciple room to continue their growth.

These new responsibilities will happen under your supervision so that you will be there to offer correction when needed and at the same time affirm what they do correctly.

Big Brother Syndrome

A word of caution. In discipleship, there is a danger of the big brother syndrome. This comes from the story of the prodigal son. After the younger son went to a distant land and squandered all of his inheritance, he came back to his senses and went back home hoping only to be accepted as a servant in his father's house. Instead, the father welcomed him back with open arms and organized a big celebration to affirm his younger son's place within the family.

When the elder brother arrived home and heard the celebration, he was angry with the father and complained about his father celebrating the return of this "ungrateful" son. He was complaining instead of celebrating. He was angry instead of welcoming the long-lost brother back into the family. He felt he deserved the attention for staying home and remaining loyal to his father unlike his younger brother.

"Big brother syndrome" is not something we like to talk about or believe exists in the church. However, this parable reminds us that there are those who have been Christians for a while but can be unwelcoming when a new believer enters the community of faith. Very few would actually say this, but these "big brothers" become very critical of the "younger brothers" and sometimes treat them with suspicion. When this behaviour is ignored, new believers feel that they are not wanted and if no one is there to walk with them in their new faith, they might even go back to the life they had before Christ.

We need to prepare our youth to know how to receive new believers well. We can disciple them by modelling ways to be welcoming and draw new people into the group. Rather than seeing these new believers as people to be suspicious of or to dismiss because of their former life, this is a discipleship opportunity for our youth who are farther along in their own spiritual journeys. We can reimagine for them the role of the big brother or sister done well.

When we use the big brother or sister idea well, young Christians will be surrounded by loving and caring believers they can look up to and they will be encouraged to continue on in their journey of faith. However, whenever we misuse this opportunity, we will likely cause significant damage to the faith of these young believers and ultimately to the Church as well.

Where Do We Start

At the beginning of Acts, the disciples were told to go to Jerusalem and wait there for the promised gift of the Holy Spirit. The power of the Holy Spirit was going to enable them to be God's witnesses "in Jerusalem, and in all Judea and Samaria, and to the ends of the earth" (Acts 1:8). This was the command Jesus gave to His disciples, and we can learn some lessons here about where we should start.

New believers need faithful living testimonies who can serve as examples for them as they walk the discipleship journey.

First, the disciples obeyed the instruction to wait in a certain place in order to receive the Holy Spirit. To be an effective disciple and discipler, we have to have an obedient spirit whereby we become sensitive to the voice of God and we live ready to follow His instruction. Each one of us has been instructed to make disciples of all nations, and in order to do that we must be willing to obey God's instruction. It is through our obedience that God can use us to greatly impact our world for the kingdom of God.

Secondly, the disciples were united in purpose. They obeyed and were united in the purpose of God's mission. They were to share in the mission of taking the gospel to every known part of the world, and they were united in their desire to accomplish what was ahead of them. As believers today, when we set out to do discipleship, we must be united in this same purpose. This means being intentional about how we do discipleship and having a willingness to disciple whomever God sends our way.

The third aspect of this is simply the witness of the disciples. After the Holy Spirit came upon them, they did not keep the message to themselves. They went out to share the good news of Jesus and the power of His resurrection. As believers, we have been called to be witnesses. We are first-hand witnesses of what God is doing and has done in our lives. The world desperately needs faithful living testimonies who can give witness to the transformative power of Jesus in a surrendered life. Likewise, new believers need faithful living testimonies who can serve as examples for them as they walk the discipleship journey.

Above all, we cannot do discipleship in our strength. The Holy Spirit is our guide, and the Holy Spirit is the one who enables us to be faithful and authentic disciples. Ask God to fill you with the Holy Spirit so you can grow in your own walk and be a faithful guide to the next generation of believers. Discipleship is an exciting journey. Let's make sure we are bringing others along.

CHAPTER 3

Discipleship:
Being Formed Through the Spiritual Disciplines

Milton Gay

Milton Gay is the Regional NYI Coordinator for Mesoamerica and a missionary who serves in Guatemala. Youth ministry is exciting to him because there is a new generation with passion for the Lord and His work. Discipleship is important to Milton because it transforms the lives of youth and makes them into disciples of Christ.

Discipline is not a popular word. In general, most of us like being able to do whatever we want to do whenever we feel like doing it, and our youth are just like us. However, if we are honest with ourselves, we will acknowledge how rapidly the glamor of self-indulgence can wear off and the negative consequences can start to accumulate. Life requires discipline, and our spiritual lives do as well. In his first letter to the Corinthians, Paul reminds them about the need for self-discipline. "Do you not know that in a race all the runners run, but only one gets the prize? Run in such a way as to get the prize. Everyone who competes in the games goes into strict training. They do it to get a crown that will not last, but we do it to get a crown that will last forever. Therefore, I do not run like someone running aimlessly; I do not fight like a boxer beating the air. No, I strike a blow to my body and make it my slave so that after I have preached to others, I myself will not be disqualified for the prize" (1 Corinthians 9:24-27).

> ...we must be honest with ourselves and ask whether our discipleship strategies are fostering "rigid formalism" or "sentimental romanticism" or whether we are truly helping the seed of faith planted in our youth grow deep roots.

The Christian life takes intentional effort to live rightly and to grow as a disciple of Jesus Christ. Scripture often uses words like training, endurance, and discipline to communicate this key aspect of our faith. According to Henri Nouwen in his book *Spiritual Formation*, "Discipleship, however, calls for discipline. Indeed, discipleship and discipline share the same linguistic root (from *discere*, which means 'to learn from'), and the two should never be separated. Whereas discipline without discipleship leads to rigid formalism, discipleship without discipline ends in sentimental romanticism." As we consider the ways we seek to disciple our youth, we must be honest with ourselves and ask whether our discipleship strategies are fostering "rigid formalism" or "sentimental romanticism" or whether we are truly helping the seed of faith planted in our youth grow deep roots.

In this chapter, we are going to discuss discipleship through the engagement of the spiritual disciplines. The spiritual disciplines we are going to discuss in this chapter are Bible reading, prayer, worship, fasting, silence, simplicity, service, and journaling. First we will explore why youth need to be practicing these spiritual disciplines, then we will review what our role is as a discipler in this process, and finally we will end with practical suggestions for how to incorporate these disciplines into our youth ministries.

The Spiritual Disciplines and Youth

In his book, *Celebration of Discipline*, Richard Foster says that the spiritual disciplines are "a way of sowing for the Spirit. The Disciplines are God's way of getting us into the ground; they put us where He can work within us and transform us."[2] They are exercises or practices that support our spiritual growth and allow us to grow in maturity and Christlikeness. Discipleship is the process by which we learn about the Christian life until we are made into the likeness of Christ. The need for this level of openness to the work of God in our lives is no less necessary for youth. In some ways it is even more significant because if youth embrace these disciplines when they are young, they are more likely to become central components to their faith into young adulthood and beyond. Let's look at five reasons why youth need to be intentionally practicing spiritual disciplines.

The spiritual disciplines provide a faithful call back to be who God created [our youth] to be and to allow their character to be formed by God.

To live free from sin and enjoy a life of holiness

The only way to be free from sin and to live a life of holiness is to ask Jesus to be our Savior and to allow space for Christ to be formed in us through discipleship. The spiritual disciplines call us to participate in counter-cultural practices in order to make space for such formation to take place. For youth who are pulled in so many directions, these disciplines ground them in Christ and keep them oriented on the things of God.

To connect with God

As with any relationship, our relationship with God needs regular and focused times for connection. Those times should include honest sharing and attentive listening. The spiritual life is built through daily practices and keeps us connected with our inexhaustible source of power and love. Many youth struggle to feel known and loved just as they are. Learning how to listen to God and receive God's unconditional love is a transformative and life-giving connection in their lives.

To know the peace of restored relationship

Sin breaks all relationships, but the grace and power of Christ reconnects us with love, peace, and hope. For youth, having friendships and a sense of belonging is vitally important. As youth learn what it means to be in right relationship with God, they will be healthier individuals in their relationships with others as well.

To form character

God shapes and transforms our lives and our characters through the spiritual disciplines. Romans 12:2 calls us to not conform to the pattern of this world or a mediocre life, but to be transformed by God. Youth are working their way through the challenging task of discovering who they are. They try on identities and attitudes like clothes. The spiritual disciplines provide a faithful call back to be who God created them to be and to allow their character to be formed by God.

To be shaped as a leader

A faithful spiritual leader is someone who seeks after God and depends on God and His grace rather than his or her own charisma and talents. As youth are invited into leadership, there should be accountability regarding their engagement with the various spiritual disciplines. We want our youth to be leaders who have deep relationships with Jesus, who serve and worship with God's people, who pray continually, and who lead a life of integrity before God and others.

Discipleship as Spiritual Mentoring

As we prepare to help our youth begin or more faithfully practice the spiritual disciplines, we need to be acutely aware of our own role as a "spiritual mentor" of sorts. As disciplers of youth, we must be willing to offer all our knowledge and experience in service to them, to support their own spiritual formation and growth. Here are three reminders of our role in this journey.

Stay close to their reality

We are facing the greatest technological phenomenon in history, as cell phones, tablets, and computers are no longer just accessories for youth to carry but have become an extension of their bodies. The excessive exposure to and use of mass media and the internet has changed the attention spans of young people around the world because now everything is accessible with just a click. Our youth are now exposed to life-altering sin at such a young age, and many have lost interest in matters of faith and have renounced any belief in God.

As believers seeking to disciple the next generation, what should we do? We must be in touch with their reality. We need to talk with them and listen to their struggles, fears, and temptations. During these conversations, our talking needs to be kept to a minimum. Listen, listen, listen. Additionally, even when we stop talking, we need to make sure we are modeling the life of a disciple of Jesus Christ.

Walk with them

As we work to disciple youth, we must be prepared to invest our lives in them and offer our help as we walk with them. It is not easy. Our responsibility as we disciple youth is to accompany them along their spiritual journeys from unbelief to mature faith. These spiritual journeys will have many highs and many lows. Perhaps the most important thing for us to remember, especially during the lows, is our call to provide our youth with a real life, face-to-face example of the unconditional love of Christ.

Trust God to transform them

This is crucial. We *do not* have the power to change anyone's life. We listen to them, we walk with them, but only God can transform them. Our criticizing or nagging will likely do more harm than good. Pray regularly for your youth and entrust them to God. Pray for God to give you the right words to say at the right time but pray for the Holy Spirit to be at work in their hearts and lives.

As leaders, we must do our part to prepare "the soil" where God is wanting to work in the lives of our youth. This includes having activities they can relate to and find significant to help them connect to the work of the church. It also means we challenge them to practice the spiritual disciplines in order to grow and transform.

Finally, I want to end this section with a story. Eight years ago, I met a young man whose appearance did not look promising. I did not think that he would become a good leader because I did not see any innate qualities in him. In fact, the way he lived was not what we would call "Christian," which was confirmed by his conduct. Over time, as we worked with him through the spiritual disciplines which are practiced and modeled as part of the certificate in Youth Ministry we have on the Mesoamerica Region, his life turned around. God completely transformed his life, and he began to serve as a youth leader in his local church, then on his district. Today he is the lead pastor of one of the churches with the most youth and membership on his district. Now he guides teens and youth through the means of grace, blessing others by sharing his faith and the other spiritual practices.

[Spiritual disciplines] are not an end in themselves but a means to help us find Christ and live into the grace of God amidst a superficial, undisciplined society that is indifferent to God.

These spiritual disciplines are essential if we want our youth to take seriously the call to become disciples of Christ. Let's explore how God can use us to lead youth to experience the grace of God though these practices.

Practicing the Spiritual Disciplines

Spiritual disciplines are also known as means of grace. Practicing them keeps us connected with our Creator. They are not an end in themselves but a means to help us find Christ and live into the grace of God amidst a superficial, undisciplined society that is indifferent to God. For John Wesley and the Methodists, the spiritual disciplines were essential. They prayed constantly and enjoyed an ordered and disciplined life of holiness which gave them an identity and left a historical heritage for those of us who follow their traditions and beliefs. In one of his sermons, John Wesley spoke of the means of grace in this way, "By 'means of grace' I understand outward signs, words, or actions, ordained of God, and appointed for this end, to be the ordinary channels whereby he might convey to [us], preventing, justifying, or sanctifying grace."[3]

As we discuss the various spiritual disciplines, be thinking about how you could intentionally incorporate these practices into your youth gatherings, how you could incorporate them into your own life, and how you could call your youth to do the same. Each section will end with some ideas for putting that discipline into practice. I encourage you to pick several examples and make plans to help your youth develop these disciplines.

Reading the Word

In his pastoral letter to Timothy, the Apostle Paul (who was Timothy's mentor and discipler) wrote to advise him that he should treasure the reading of Scripture, because "All Scripture is God-breathed and is useful for teaching, rebuking, correcting and training in righteousness, so that the servant of God may be thoroughly equipped for every good work" (2 Timothy 3:16-17).

While we use the Bible regularly in our youth gatherings and Sunday School classes, we must be intentional to help our youth come to understand the whole story of God and the way He is at work in our world. We need to ask ourselves if our youth are growing up and leaving our youth ministry with only an understanding of the "top 10" Bible stories but without knowing how the whole Bible weaves together into the main story of God's love of creation. Getting to know the whole story allows youth to see the Bible as more than just a rule book or a collection of short stories. Recognizing how God has been at work in the world before teaches us to look for how God is at work in our world today and how He calls us to join Him.

Therefore, we must help our youth learn how to read the Bible and help them understand the idea of it being a discipline. Allowing God's Word to shape us requires more than quickly reading a couple of verses as we run out the door for the day. Provide times for your youth to practice engaging with Scripture in these four different ways:

1. **Read it.** Have them still their hearts and mind in preparation to read the Bible. Invite them to begin by praying to God and asking for wisdom to understand what they are about to read and how to apply it to their lives.

2. **Meditate on it.** Have your youth spend time reflecting, thinking, and finding the purpose of the passage they have read. Scripture must be received, meditated on, and treasured in the heart so it can become incarnated and penetrate into the deepest parts of our being.

3. **Live it out.** Have them explore how God might be asking them to live out the lessons of this passage. Challenge them to plan for the actions they will need to take in order be obedient to God in regards to this passage.

4. **Share it.** This might be the scariest one for youth, but once we have started living out the Scriptures, we are ready to share the good news with others. Provide space for your youth to present a short devotional, teach a Sunday School class, or lead a Bible study. Sharing what they have learned will serve to further ground its truth in their hearts.

Putting It Into Practice:

- Form small groups to meet during the week and read together in a group.
- Encourage youth to use readily available apps to maintain daily contact with God's Word.
- Incorporate a Scripture journaling time in your youth gatherings where youth can write about what they are hearing in the Scripture text that week.

Prayer

Prayer is simply a conversation with God. For John Wesley, prayer was a means of grace because he believed God made Himself present in prayer, a time when we present ourselves before God and break into the supernatural. God is listening to us and is among us. In *The Upward Call* we read, "[Prayer] is an ongoing relationship, a continual dialogue with the Heavenly Father. Prayer at this level becomes as natural as breathing."[4]

However, many youth (and adults too) struggle with both corporate and private prayer. It is important to not dismiss their fears and struggles but be open with youth about our own struggles and help them grow in this area of their Christian life. We want them to come to see how prayer is a vital part of the Christian life. It is through prayer that we encounter our Lord, whom we love and trust. Prayer brings change, transformation, liberation, healing, holiness, and hope.

In your youth gatherings, invite youth to lead times of prayer, but ask them in advance and if they have concerns, talk with them about it. Let them know that it is okay to write out their prayers. Provide space for your youth to pray silently. Have times when you lift up prayers of intercession. Work to make sure your youth gatherings are safe spaces for youth to practice praying.

Putting It Into Practice:

· Teach the youth that there are different ways of communicating with God. For some it is easy to pray spontaneously and eloquently, while others can express themselves better by writing out their prayers.
· Go to places where personal and community prayer needs are posted.
· Encourage them to join in prayer at a specific time no matter where they are, to strengthen their sense of togetherness.
· Teach them to give public testimony when they receive an answer to prayer from God.

Worship

In worship we receive the grace and hope of God from being in communion with other believers, united in worship to God with our hearts, souls, and bodies. In worship we rejoice and participate in the songs of praise we lift up to God, the offerings we present, the preaching of the Word, the Lord's Supper, the times of fellowship, the prayers we pray, and the confessions we offer up. When we think of worship to God, we need to make sure we are thinking more broadly than just the time of singing.

Perhaps the most common pitfall we need to help our youth guard against is the danger of entering lightly into worship. Worship is not an act or show. We do not approach worship as simple spectators, without showing gratitude, participating, or truly worshiping. Sometimes we just assume that if our youth are singing, they are worshiping. However, discipleship through the spiritual discipline of worship means that we are not only practicing worship with our youth, but we are teaching about it as well.

As we prepare for worship, we need to consider how we can help our youth engage meaningfully in it. We also need to help our youth see their whole lives as worship to God. Worship goes beyond the time of corporate singing during a church service. Our lives are to be lived as an act of worship to God.

Putting It Into Practice:

- Involve young people in the liturgy of the worship service.
- Teach them and challenge them to preach, teach, give offerings, and worship through song.
- Take time to prepare together for worship prior to the service.
- Regularly challenge your youth to view their whole lives as acts of worship to God.

Fasting

Fasting involves denying ourselves in order to grow closer to God and grow in His grace. Fasting is learning to depend on God more than food and keeping us focused on our relationship with God above all else.

While fasting can be done together at church or in a time of retreat with our youth, it should never be forced, and the physical needs of our youth must be respected. It should also never be done in a way that is manipulative of our youth or the will of God. When done appropriately, these times can open up unique opportunities for God to touch the lives of our youth.

Fasting can go beyond food. In the midst of a noisy and superficial world, encourage your youth to set times to abstain from the excessive use of technology and social media. These things often separate us from being in communion with God. Many youth dedicate hours a day to communicating with their friends but neglect their communication and relationship with the Lord.

Putting It Into Practice:

- Organize a group fast to offer yourselves together as a living and holy sacrifice.
- Teach youth the right meaning of the discipline of fasting.
- Choose some activities where you refrain from using social media as a group to devote your time to worship and prayer to God.

Silence

Silence is to refrain from interacting with others and to be still so that we can listen to God and find His will for our lives. As we mentioned in the previous section, we live in a noisy world. The discipline of silence calls us to seek out a place where you can experience solitude and silence without any of those distractions and completely focus on being with and seeking God.

Let's be honest, this discipline will be weird, uncomfortable, and even scary for some of our youth. However, when we are alone in the presence of God meditating on Scripture, it begins to not only speak to us but takes root in our life, drawing us to the Father in a wonderful way and building a dwelling for Him in us.

I attended my first silent retreat a few years ago. In the beginning it was the most tedious and boring thing I had ever done, because I am an energetic and fiery person who gets energized by talking. Locking myself in a bedroom was very frustrating at first, but after thirty minutes I began to experience something extraordinary which changed my life, and now I practice the discipline of silence regularly.

Putting It Into Practice:

- Organize a spiritual retreat where you can combine several spiritual disciplines to practice with your youth ministry.
- Give youth the opportunity to enjoy silence in the presence of God.
- Encourage them to have personal retreats for spiritual renewal.
- Gather your leadership team at least once a year to hold a spiritual retreat and seek God.

Simplicity

In his book *Celebration of Discipline* Richard Foster says, "Simplicity sets us free to receive provision of God as a gift that is not ours to keep and can be freely shared with others."[5] We have to help youth understand the discipline of stewarding what God has provided without opulence or legalism, simply learning to seek God's kingdom and justice, and trusting all else to be added.

To live simply means being content when we have little or when we have more than what we need. Simplicity calls us to live our lives seeking opportunities to share our possessions, our time, and our abilities with others. We are only able to live this way when we recognize that everything we have comes from God and we are sustained by God and not our own striving.

It is especially easy for youth to find their identity in their possessions and to depend on technology, fashion, or other material items to express who they are. This discipline also calls us to find the fullness of our identity in Christ alone.

Putting It Into Practice:

- Organize youth gatherings with a focus on simplicity.
- Provide opportunities for youth to share what they have with others.
- As a youth leader, be a model of humility and simplicity.

Service

As we surrender our lives to God, we begin to move from being egocentric to thinking of others first. Loving God means that we must show love to our neighbors, and only then can we make a difference in our churches, communities, schools, universities and homes. God has given us gifts so that we might serve others and be able to share His grace.

When we serve those in need, we are fulfilling the purpose for which God allowed Phineas F. Bresee to establish the Church of the Nazarene: to minister to the poor and needy. The denomination's first churches were a living testimony of this purpose. Likewise, for John Wesley, holiness was social. That is, we cannot live holiness privately or only inside the church. We must go out and express it through service to others.

As we disciple our youth, we need to challenge them to daily seek out opportunities to serve as this is not a practice reserved for organized service days. Those are important, but service is a lifestyle where we learn to give without expecting anything in return, serving with joy in our hearts.

Putting It Into Practice:

- Motivate your youth to help their parents and siblings at home.
- Guide them to visit, pray for, and do works of mercy for the elderly, for orphans, and those in hospitals.
- Involve them in serving the local church in different ministries.

Journaling

Writing in a journal is nothing new, and some of your youth might already have a similar practice. John Wesley kept a journal and encouraged his disciples to do so as well in order to keep a record of their encounters with God. Journaling is powerful way to help you see your growth in Christ. It is something that is simple but carries great significance because through it you can meet the Lord. You can start by taking notes on your smartphone, devoting time daily to write about God's blessings and your life story.

Journaling can provide the opportunity for focused reflection and response for those who aren't comfortable speaking out loud in a group setting. Try incorporating times of journaling during a Bible lesson or youth gathering to allow your youth to record what they are learning and what God is saying to them.

Putting It Into Practice:

- Challenge your youth to keep a personal journal where they detail their day-to-day experiences.
- Develop a guide with verses and thoughts for reflection to guide and help youth to write down their experiences.

Journeying With Your Youth

Many writers agree that discipleship with the spiritual disciplines is a journey of spiritual formation. However, in undertaking this wonderful adventure, we need to have companions for the trip; companions who will help us and whom we can help. We cannot just challenge our youth to embrace these disciplines, we must be living them out in our own lives as well.

By themselves, the disciplines are not the most important element in the journey, because they are only a means by which the grace of God flows. The most important element in this journey is God. God is the reason why we embrace these disciplines, incarnate them, and teach them to new generations of young people. If you choose to take this journey, you and your youth will end up as free, faithful, and willing children of God who are prepared for every good work.

CHAPTER 4

Discipleship in Groups: Discovering the Advantages of Formative Communities

Nabil Habiby

Nabil Habiby is a youth leader who serves in Beirut, Lebanon. Youth ministry is exciting to him because he can see youth at the beginning of a long journey of discovering and engaging with God. Nabil believes that discipleship is important because without it, all of our programs, talks, games, and camps are almost useless.

"And he went up on the mountain and called to him those whom he desired, and they came to him. And he appointed twelve (whom he also named apostles) so that they might be with him and he might send them out to preach." (Mark 3:13-14, ESV)

Defining our Terms and Mapping the Way

What do we mean by a "discipleship group?"

In this chapter we will discuss how to do discipleship among youth in groups. Before we do that, it is important to define the term "discipleship group." First, whenever we use the term "discipleship group" we will be talking about a set number of people. This number, as we will see, can be small or big, but it is a stable number. Secondly, a discipleship group is a set number of people who meet regularly. Again, they might meet once every three days or every three months, but their meetings are regular. Finally, a discipleship group in this chapter is a set number of people who meet regularly and in the same place or geographical area. This does not have to be in the same actual space. They could meet once in the church, another time in a local café, and a third time in someone's home. However, they are still in the same area. Hence, whenever we talk about group discipleship in this chapter, we will be talking about a set number of people who meet regularly in the same place.

Why form groups?

Why are groups, small or big, important? First of all, Jesus himself formed a group of twelve disciples. He probably experienced varying degrees of intimacy with each member, but all in all the group was twelve. Secondly, our very human nature seeks fellowship; a deep sense of being in communion with others. Thirdly, learning — an important aspect of discipleship — happens in innovative ways in groups. Finally, our Christian faith is, in its essence, a love relationship with a Triune God — a God who is a loving relationship of three persons — and with each other. Discipleship in groups gives one the chance to learn about and live out her/his Christian faith in practical and creative ways.

Where shall we go now?

How shall we then go about exploring discipleship in groups? We shall be guided by the size of the group. Hence, the first part will discuss groups of two, the second part will discuss small groups, and the third part will discuss the entire church as a group. Every section will include instructions on how to form such a group, advice on how discipleship can happen in it, warning of the potential pitfalls, a list of the advantages of this group size, and a few reflection questions at the end. The words below stem from 10 years of personal experience in church, NGO (non-governmental organization), and school ministry among youth. I pray that my humble suggestions will be a catalyst for an increased interest and commitment in discipleship. Enough then with introductions; let's get to it!

Part 1: The Cherished Friendship — Groups of Two

How are they formed?

We start with the basic group, two people. How does this group form? The first thought that comes to mind is, "how will I be able to choose who to be close friends with?" You might have 10 or 100 attendees in your youth group, but it will be almost impossible to form a one-on-one discipleship group with each and every one of them. Here are two tips to help you choose.

First, leave it up to the natural flow of things. Sometimes circumstances (God's hand perhaps?) push some youth towards you. Maybe it's the youth you have to drive home for 30 minutes after every meeting. Or maybe it's the teenager who is your neighbour. Perhaps it's the young girl who you happen to see every week at the mall. Whichever the case, keep an open heart (and schedule) to teenagers which you feel God is urging you to personally mentor. I remember one time I was praying for wisdom to choose who to disciple on a one-on-one basis, and the next week one of the teenagers who attends the school where I work came up to me and said, "I want to meet with you once per month." Well, all right God, I get it. Things probably won't be this straightforward, but stay alert.

Secondly, leave it up to chemistry. Chances are a teenager who does not like you that much will not be too happy with the idea of having you as her/his personal mentor. You hopefully have 5 leaders to a group of 30 teenagers. Which of these 30 are closer to you? With whom do you click? Who seems to gravitate to you? Or, conversely, who is that teenager who is always alone and does not click with anyone? In both cases, when a person connects with you or when a youth is in need of a friend, you should probably step in and establish a one-on-one discipleship relationship with that person.

How does discipleship happen?

You form this friendship with a youth. Great. Now what? How does discipleship happen? Let me start off by saying that I have yet to have a good experience with a "set" discipleship curriculum in one-on-one situations. You might have an excellent curriculum, or your experience might be different than mine. Great, use it. I would prefer that discipleship in one-on-one discipleship groups happen in three ways.

First, discipleship occurs over informal discussions. Your conversation over dinner could start with school and the weather but end with sex and the Bible. Some of the most enriching conversations have happened between me and teenagers while I was *taking them home* after our regular meal or walk together. I've found myself discussing dating, masturbation, the difference between the Bible and the Qur'an, and a host of other challenging topics after the "casual" conversation had been exhausted. As this mentoring relationship gets built, this teenager you are meeting with regularly soon starts to open up the challenging spiritual discussions from the beginning of your time together.

> **Be it a set curriculum, informal discussions, times of emergency, or during everyday ministry, all are chances to share life and hopefully help her/him and yourself become more like Christ.**

Secondly, other than informal discussions, as you build this friendship, you might start getting "emergency calls" asking for help in certain issues. They might not literally call you, but it is in urgent times that you have a chance to connect at a deeper level with your young disciple. The fact that this teenager has called you first after her father has kicked her out of the house is a sign of great trust. Now, I am definitely *not* saying you should cause a crisis in order to step in and be a listening ear, but as you build a relationship with the youth, be ready to step in and step up when the time comes.

Finally, other than informal discussions and times of crisis, I have found that taking your young disciple along to do ministry opens up new levels of spiritual and social growth. Bring him along as you do a house visit, distribute food portions to the needy, prepare your Sunday order of worship, or clean the church basement. Let her/him be an active member of the kingdom of God (even if she/he still does not understand what this Kingdom is). I had a great relationship with a young man who used to be a student at the school. He graduated our middle school but would still show up at my office every few weeks to discuss theology and life. I started to take him along as I did house visits to refugee families around the church. These were precious times where our relationship was strengthened, and we were able to discuss the meaning of the Christian life in practical ways. This young man has chosen to become a clergy member in a traditional church, and I look forward in anticipation to see him ministering to the people of Beirut as a priest.

Be it a set curriculum, informal discussions, times of emergency, or during everyday ministry, all are chances to share life and hopefully help her/him and yourself become more like Christ. However, a few words of caution are in order.

What are the dangers of one-on-one discipleship groups?

Having a close discipleship group with a teenager is not without its pitfalls. First, you must be wary of the way other youth vying for your attention view this. Will they feel envy? Does it look like special treatment? In Lebanon you usually invite all of your friends to your weddings. I took the decision not to invite any student from the school to my wedding. However, I did invite a few youth who had graduated from school and whom I was discipling. A few months after my wedding, I learned that a few of the youth at school were grumbling because they had missed out on my wedding. As you build a close relationship with one teenager, another one is probably gazing with disgruntlement as Joseph receives his coloured robe. To counter this, work with the other youth leaders or adults in your church and encourage them to be intentional about mentoring other youth. Do your best to make sure all of the teenagers have some leader who is discipling them in this way.

Secondly, and I can't stress this enough, mixed gender one-on-one disciple-ship is a disaster waiting to happen. Why? Spending time on a regular basis with a person of the opposite gender, particularly if that person is a teen-ager, opens up the way for unethical behaviour. In fact, even if the person is from the same gender, be wary of developing an unhealthy relationship of dependency where the young disciple looks up to you to solve all their prob-lems, idolization where she/he thinks that you are perfect, or substitution, where you gradually take the place of their family and friends. But, fear not, these one-on-one discipleship groups also offer some amazing advantages.

What are the advantages of one-on-one discipleship groups?

The first advantage is that one-on-one discipleship groups allow you to move beyond the first level of Christian ministry where you simply proclaim or share truths of the Kingdom with a teenager. As you build this relation-ship, you will be able to discuss, share, and be challenged by the Kingdom in new and refreshing ways. As trust deepens, so do the conversations; lifelong change can and does happen.

Secondly, these close friendships usually last beyond teenage years. My wife's eyes still sparkle every time she sees her teenage mentor. As your young disciple moves into adulthood, you might just find yourself becom-ing best friends on a whole new level. Conversely, if communication stops, you might be surprised one night with a phone call from your old disciple asking for advice, wanting to meet up, or simply saying hello.

One-on-one discipleship groups are beautiful. Isn't the Christian life in its essence a walk of two, Christ with each one of us? Yes, we walk together as a collective body of believers, but to be able to walk together in a loving way we must be walking personally with Christ. What is a two-person disciple-ship group then? It is a challenge, an invitation to be Christ who walks with a teenager and to see Christ in the teenager with whom you are walking. Discover the Kingdom together!

Part 2 — The Familiarity of Fellowship: Small groups (3 to 12 people)

How are they formed?

We now move to the more familiar territory of small groups. How are they formed? From my experience, they are formed from two different scenarios:

a common activity or a common attribute. First, you might find that in your youth group a number of teenagers all share the same interest. A while ago a friend introduced me to the wonderful game of Settlers of Catan (no, this is not a paid advert). Soon, five of my youth also became addicted. We were meeting every two weeks to play Catan. There you have it, folks: a group was formed. It was not yet an official discipleship group, but when you have worked with teenagers for some time you realize that it is precious to find a small group who meets every week. This group can easily be turned into a Catan-inspired discipleship group. Another example are three teenagers who all like to eat. (Who doesn't?!) A year ago, we started to go out on a monthly basis to try a new restaurant. While we are eating, our discussions have taken us all over life, including what it means to follow God today. A final example is a drama-themed discipleship group which my wife led with a group of 10 teenagers. They all loved drama, and they all wanted to discover the Bible.

Secondly, the group might be brought together by common attributes. They might all be the same age, live in the same area, or share some other common attribute. They naturally feel comfortable together. Now, be aware that small groups should also challenge the comfort zone of the teenagers and their perception of "us" and "them." However, you might find that through common interests or attributes a group has already formed without any inorganic effort on your behalf.

Let me stress, however, that to start an official discipleship group the leader has to take the initiative. As we saw above, a group might form naturally, but for it to become a discipleship group, the leader has to step in. I have always found that putting a set time to meet regularly gives a certain seriousness to the group and helps the leader do discipleship in an effective manner.

How does discipleship happen?

You form a small group for discipleship, but unlike the discipleship group of two, leaving discipleship up to informal talk or times of crisis won't bring about positive results. I am not saying that you should turn your group into a strict class, but creating a healthy routine and structure will pay dividends in terms of discipleship. Here, I strongly advise the leader to either use a set curriculum (get one or create one) or set the topic for the meeting. You might want to discuss something in a laid-back setting using the Bible every now and then but do set a topic. I tend to do an open question-answer session once every four times which breaks the routine and gives a chance for the youth to freely express themselves. When a teenager hits me with a question out of the blue, I can deftly reply with "note it down for our next question-answer session." Let me add that it is vital to explore a Bible passage together every time. This might happen through drama, discussion, videos, or other creative ways, but teenagers should become familiar with the Bible, if for no other reason than the fact that one day they will leave your group. If they don't know how to read the Bible (or enjoy the Bible) then your efforts will have been in vain!

Informal discussions play a role in discipleship. They tend to happen on the fringes while you mingle at the beginning, wait for one late member, drop them off to their homes, or while you chat over social media. It is in these spaces *around* the official discipleship time that informal discussions will help you delve deeper with your small group. While I argued above that you should relegate off-topic questions to a question-answer session, sometimes you should follow the rabbit trail even if it means you won't be able to finish all you wanted to cover.

If ministering together in one-on-one discipleship groups is an option, then doing ministry with a small group is almost obligatory. In a small group you have 3-12 energy-filled teenagers who are learning what it means to be part of the kingdom of God. Well, news flash, the Kingdom is not only sitting around a table and reading the Bible. There's a small group I know who goes once every two months to a local NGO to fill food packages. Our local children's program is run by a few "adults" and a group of teenagers who are being discipled. The committee which helps me lead the youth ministry at my local church is equally made up of adult leaders and discipled teenagers. The opportunities are infinite. Pity the church or community who does not invest in its committed small groups for the work of the Kingdom. However, not all is a breeze, and small groups have their fair share of dangers.

What are the dangers of small groups?

First, while introverts blossom in one-on-one discipleship groups, most will refrain from talking in small groups. This is naturally more pronounced in small groups which are larger than six people. Be careful as you lead the group that it does not turn into a group of eight participants and four spectators. Here the role of creativity in approaching the Bible passage and in doing ministry together will be important in making sure the introverts of the group participate.

Secondly, another pitfall of small groups is making the choice to accept/reject members. Do you ask late-comers (last 15 minutes) to wait outside as to not disrupt the flow of the discussion, or do you welcome them? What do you do with teenagers who are not always there? How about spiritual level? Do you handpick the participants of your group or leave it open to whoever wants to walk in? Each of these choices have their advantages and disadvantages. I, and probably others, do not have easy answers. What I can say is that you have to do what ensures that those attending the group actually get discipled. Just like one-on-one discipleship groups, some youth will feel "left out" and might even resent those who are in a discipleship group. But, be careful of creating a mentality of hierarchy whereby those who are part of a group appear to be holier or higher than the "common people" who simply attend youth meetings.

Not only are there the dangers of non-participation from some members and the formation of exclusive groups, small groups can also deteriorate in a few days when two members get into a fight. One such discipleship group, made up of six males, was going strong for over two years, then two of the boys had a bitter fight. One left, the others took sides, and the once-strong discipleship group started looking rather worn. I don't think there is a way to avoid such situations. This is part of life. However, you can be proactive as a leader by stepping in early and trying to bring reconciliation or perhaps, in extreme cases, ask both parties to take a break from the group. At the end of the day, if we can't learn how to resolve conflict peacefully in a discipleship group in a church setting, then where else can we do that?

One final danger is that the small discipleship group becomes a replica of the Sunday service. You should not spend 30 minutes giving a "sermon" in a discipleship group. Think about your small discipleship group more as a Bible study for youth. You meet to explore the Bible, to talk about the Kingdom, and then to go out and be the Kingdom. Sunday church is amazing, but it is not a small discipleship group.

In summary then, be wary of isolating introverts, rejecting/accepting some members, intra-group conflict, and the replication of the regular Sunday service. Enough warnings; now let us move to the positives.

What are the advantages of small groups?

First, deep talks can and do happen in small groups. You might see some teenagers for five years and never have a deep talk with them. However, you spend time with them in a structured small group discipleship setting and soon you are discussing entire sanctification in the Wesleyan revival! If you are faithful in preparing creative ways to engage with the Bible, deep talks are bound to happen.

Secondly, friendships are built. Soon enough you might find that the group enjoys going out on a fun outing outside the discipleship schedule. Friendships created in this small group setting may also last a lifetime.

Finally, rejoice, for the small group is a model of what the early church looked like. Biblical scholars agree that the early church in the Roman world was probably a house church. Small groups met to read the Scriptures, share the teachings of the apostles, and have a communion meal together. They were also groups of support for each other, as evidenced in the first chapters of Acts, where the rich shared what they had with the poor. So, as you come together with your small group of teenagers to discuss the word of God and live out the Kingdom, be merry, for you are engaging in an ancient living practice. The early church transformed continents. Who knows what your group will do!

If you are faithful in preparing creative ways to engage with the Bible, deep talks are bound to happen.

Part 3 — The Joyful Gathering: Church group (13-50 people)

How are they formed?

Some readers might object to the entire church youth group being placed under the heading of discipleship groups. I retort with a question: Does discipleship happen during the regular "big" meeting? I think it does. But before we move to exploring how it happens, let us discuss how this church group is formed. There are a myriad of resources online and in hard copy on how to create a youth meeting. I will then briefly note that a church group is built by inviting teenagers to the group, when the regular church-goers bring their children to the group, and when a regular meeting time for the group is respected. This last one is critical because a teenager who shows up to find the church closed will probably refrain from coming again. I will make do with this short introduction and jump right into the question of discipleship in a big group.

How does discipleship happen?

First, discipleship happens in the traditional ways of listening to a sermon or Bible study, prayer, and worship. If the message is engaging and relevant to the youth, if the worship time is done in a creative and faithful manner, then yes, these usually "boring" aspects of the meeting can become moments of discipleship where the youth gain new realizations, make lifelong decisions, and fall more in love with Jesus.

Similar to the two other group types, discipleship also happens during the informal times of the meeting. This is usually the mingling at the beginning and the end (around food, naturally), game time, and while the leaders drive the youth to and from the church. As we have already discussed above, such times pave the way for the formation of small groups or one-on-one groups of discipleship. Conducting a meeting with perfect (read: crazy and engaging) content but failing to spend time chatting with the youth is almost useless! Please, do not be busy every second of the program preparing the games. Allow some leaders to walk among the teens and interact with them. Snack time is not time for the leaders to gang together and joke about their week. This is precious time for mini-discipleship to happen: relationships are strengthened, care is shown, and life is exchanged. These mini-discipleship times may even be the most important times!

Finally, and you must be expecting this by now, discipleship in the church group happens as we do ministry together. One year, in partnership with Youth For Christ Lebanon, we took our youth group during Christmas under the bridge in the slums of Beirut. We set up different posts exploring the Christmas story. Some of the teenage volunteers themselves did not know the story! It was a wonderful time of interaction with the adults and children of the area. All those involved left the place with a better understanding of the Kingdom. Another year we went up to a local NGO which takes care of street children to give them dinner and a special program. Again, some youth were not committed in their relationship with God, but they came along and saw, first-hand, what it means to be God's hand in this world.

Some youth will never be part of a small discipleship group or a one-on-one discipleship group. Some youth will daydream their way through every talk! Hence, informal times of mingling and ministry together might be the only glimpse they get of what it means to live for/with Jesus!

What are the dangers of church groups?

There are two main dangers of discipleship in church groups. First, church youth meetings can, over time, turn into a dead routine. Now, please understand that this is not to say that having a routine is bad in itself. I have been eating breakfast every day of my life, and that is a beautiful routine! I do, however, try to diversify my breakfast options to keep this healthy routine a joyful one. As you prepare for your youth meetings, ask yourself: What new things are happening in this meeting that will awake the youth to the reality of God and God's kingdom? You might not change the routine of having a sermon, but perhaps change the way the message is given. Keep the mingling time at the beginning, but perhaps paste a few challenging verses around the hall. The opportunities are endless!

Secondly, on a larger scale than the small discipleship groups, many youth will turn into mere spectators in your church meeting. Discipleship and experiencing God rarely happen as one is sitting unengaged. Again, intentionally construct your meeting so that every teenager, if they want to at least, will have the chance to engage with and learn about the Kingdom.

What are the advantages of church groups?

In opposition to the final danger listed above, new youth or those simply coming to discover what this is all about, can lay low. One-on-one interactions and small groups do not have that option. Some teenagers are still not totally convinced with this Jesus thing, or they simply do not feel like engaging with others. Church groups give them the chance to be at ease.

...the entire youth group at church provides us with a glimpse of the church at large: a bustling group of different people who unite around the person of Jesus!

Secondly, we all know that the bigger the group the more beautiful the party. Want to throw a Christmas party? Want to participate in a big ministry? Church groups give you the opportunity to go big! Having a hall packed with 40 buzzing teenagers does add an edge to any activity.

Thirdly, church groups prepare youth for "adult" life in the church. If they can sit through some songs and a talk now, they will be able to find relevance in the Sunday morning worship. If they learn what it means to be a church, then as they move beyond their teenage years it will be easier to adapt to the sometimes challenging larger body of Christ in the local church.

Finally, since youth meetings usually happen at church, the teenager will start to develop a sense of belonging to this place. While in small and one-on-one discipleship groups the teenager might build a special relationship with the group leader, here a relationship starts to be built with the place itself. If close one-on-one discipleship groups show us how to walk with Christ and if small discipleship groups provide us with spiritual support, then the entire youth group at church provides us with a glimpse of the church at large: a bustling group of different people who unite around the person of Jesus!

Conclusion

Allow me to end with a passing mention of some challenges which I think we must wrestle with as youth workers today.

We live in an age of increasing individuality. How can our discipleship groups foster community in an age where I can "connect" with everyone on my personal smartphone?

We live in an age of performance. What I do and how I do it has become the subject of my social media feed. How can our discipleship groups foster intimacy — to know that I am loved as I am before I do anything and regard-less of my performance?

Finally, we live in an age of instant solutions. How can our long-term dis-cipleship groups remind us that faith is a journey of gradual growth, and the kingdom of God starts as a mustard seed and slowly blossoms into a mighty tree?

CHAPTER 5

Holistic Discipleship:
Bringing Together Families and Faith Communities

Andrea Sawtelle

Andrea Sawtelle is a youth pastor who serves in Quincy, Massachusetts, United States. Youth ministry is exciting for her because she can watch teenagers become passionate about sharing the love of Christ beyond the church walls. Discipleship is important to Andrea because we need each other as we live out this life with Christ.

Does Youth Ministry Even Matter?

We had just returned home from a mission trip to Honduras that was incredible. We had packed in the days with endless opportunities to serve in orphanages, churches, schools, and more. Our team had ministered to close to 1,000 children, our hearts had been broken by what we had encountered, and we were changed because of that. This wasn't the first time I had taken a youth group out of the country for a mission trip, but this time was certainly different. It was different because of Sarah.

Sarah and I met during her freshman year of high school when she came to try out for my volleyball team. I was a coach at the local high school, and from the start I knew she was going to be one of those athletes I loved. She had a natural athleticism, was incredibly hard working, had a deep desire to grow as a player, and respected me as a coach. Freshman year was a great start for Sarah.

Her sophomore year, Sarah was one of the few underclassmen to make the varsity team and we figured it was going to be another year of amazing growth. Little did we know, the year would prove to be one of the most difficult. A few weeks into the season, Sarah's mom called me at my house. She started the conversation by saying, "I know you are Sarah's coach, but I also heard you were a pastor, and I just wasn't sure who else to turn to." That day I listened to a mom pour out her heart over a child who was struggling so much that she wasn't sure how to help her. That broke me.

After getting off the phone with Sarah's mom, I made it my job to pour into her as much as possible. At practice I would encourage her, talk with her, and ask her about her life. I wanted her to understand that she was loved, valued, and that God had a purpose and plan for her life. Several weeks into the season, I felt like God was pushing me to ask her to come to Honduras with our youth group. Not only did she not have a relationship with God, but she didn't even come to our church. Surprisingly, she said yes anyway. I believed with all of my heart that the experience in Honduras could change everything for her. However, I had no idea what the next nine months leading up to it would look like.

Sarah wound up in a juvenile detention center about halfway through our volleyball season. She had gotten into a dark place fast and was sitting in the midst of brokenness. She was removed from school, removed from her home, and taken from all familiarity. She struggled in the first detention center so much that she was moved to another one, this time further away from home and with more restrictions. I began to fervently pray for her, hoping God was going to break through, and holding on to what I believed to be true. She was supposed to be on that trip with us.

I spent a lot of time with Sarah during that time period. I visited her in the detention centers, sent encouraging notes, and continued to build a relationship with her family as we navigated a journey which proved to be unpredictable. In a crazy, miraculous way, that July, Sarah managed to board the plane with us and embark on a 10 day mission adventure to Honduras.

Some incredible things happened in Sarah's life on that trip. For a few brief days, she began to let down some of the walls she had built up and began to talk about some of the pain she carried with her. She allowed herself to be loved by adults and her teammates, threw herself into selfless serv-ing, and began to share pieces of her story, a story that had left her heart broken. I watched as Sarah loved on teenage girls with special needs in an orphanage that housed the abused and neglected, and I saw something come alive in her. I wept at the end of the week as Sarah got up in front of the church we had been working on and shared her story, a story that in its rawness somehow still revealed the love of Jesus. Those 10 days exceeded my expectations of what I believed God could do in the life of one teenager. Then we transitioned home.

Within a few months, Sarah was back on an unpredictable journey that would eventually lead her down a path of substance abuse, trouble with the law, and pregnancy. As I watched that journey unfold, I couldn't help but think, "Where did I go wrong with her? Why couldn't I help her? I should have done something more. Does youth ministry even matter?" These became questions that would haunt me throughout my first decade of youth ministry.

I was 24 when I took my first job as a youth pastor. Not only was I too young to drive the church van (which I later wrecked the first year of driving!), but I also had all of these misconceptions I believed to be true about youth ministry. For starters, I believed the youth pastor's job was to save the world … single handedly. It didn't matter the trauma a teen had experienced, the family system they had come from, or the lack of experience I had. At the end of the day, if a teen wasn't following Jesus, that fell on me, so I had better do everything in my power to make sure that didn't happen.

This led me to my second misconception: endless activities are the key to discipleship. I believed with my whole heart that the more pizza parties we threw, the more all-nighters we endured, and the fuller our programming was, the greater chance we had in discipling our teens. It didn't matter that we were adding a million things to their already full schedule, or that we were taking them away from their family they hardly got to spend time with anyway. After all, as long as you get them in the church, discipleship happens, right?

At least that's what I believed. I never actually stopped to ask their parents. Which brings me to my third misconception. I believed parents were to be avoided at all costs. When it came to parents, they were intimidating, a hindrance, nosey, and even the enemy at times. There was no way they could actually speak into the spiritual lives of their teens with the same power I could. After all, I was young, professionally trained in youth ministry, and full of ideas.

The Great Reality

We have all come across a myriad of teenagers within our ministries. Some have grown up in the church, some have come through our doors because someone invited them, some have come from strong faith-based homes, and others have come from family systems that are just plain broken. As youth leaders, we try to do everything in our power to make a difference, share the gospel of Jesus, and build lifelong relationships. The reality is, in the end, we still have teens walking away from their faith. After examining research from the Barna Group and the National Study of Youth and Religion, author Kara Powell talks about this very thing in her book, *Sticky Faith*. She concludes that, "40-50% of kids who graduate from a church or youth group will fail to stick with their faith in college and only 20% of college students who leave the faith planned to do so during high school. The remaining 80% intended to stick with their faith but didn't."

Whether we think we are trained professionals who are full of ideas or not, these alarming statistics should cause us to ask several questions, many of which I was asking as I watched Sarah's journey unfold before my eyes after returning from our incredible trip to Honduras. "Is what we are doing working? Where have we gone wrong? Does youth ministry matter when it comes to discipleship?"

What's the Secret?

As youth leaders, I think we would all agree that youth ministry does matter, but sometimes what we think is working isn't really working all that well. Jackie was the very first teenager I met in my first youth group. She was full of life, loved her youth leaders, loved bringing friends, asked thought-provoking questions, and was at the church whenever the doors were open. Jackie's parents also attended the church but were what you would call "nominal" Christians. After pastoring Jackie through middle and high school, she went on to attend a Christian college for four years. While Jackie had some really great experiences, she's never really allowed God to grab a hold of her heart and does not attend church anywhere either.

If parents have that heavy of an influence on their teenagers' lives, and we want to disciple teenagers to have a lasting faith, then the church has got to begin to partner with families.

Matt was a teenager who stumbled into our youth ministry in middle school. He had grown up in a "Christian" home, been around several different churches, and had a decent knowledge of the Bible. However, his family life was a mess. His parents were divorced, his mom had been married multiple times, and life had just gotten complicated. Matt was intelligent, had a desire to grow in his relationship with Jesus, and attended our church with his dad. Matt went on to graduate from a Christian college, now serves in his local church, and is getting a graduate degree in counseling. Matt has a deep love for Jesus and a desire to help others discover the same.

Becca came to our youth group as a sophomore in high school because she was dating one of our teen "church" boys. The first week I met her, I quickly learned that while she was happy to be at youth group, she really didn't have a desire to know who God was. After several months of attending, Becca not only came to love our youth group but accepted Jesus as her personal Savior. Over the next two years (even after breaking up with her boyfriend), she rose up as teen leader in our youth group, brought her dad to church, and now attends a Christian college where she is studying to be a youth pastor.

When I think about teens like Jackie, Matt, and Becca, I believe full-heartedly youth ministry has made a difference in some way or another. Yet the reality is, I have a lot more "Jackie" stories than I'd like to tell, stories of teens who fall in the 40-50% of those who will walk away from the church. While there are many factors involved with what Kara Powell calls "Sticky Faith," one of the greatest sources of influence is the family. "The National Study of Youth and Religion concluded that the best way for youth to become more serious about religious faith is for parents to become more serious about theirs."[2] Powell goes on to boldly state in her own book, "When it comes to kids' faith, parents get what they are."[3] In other words, how parents choose to live out their own faith has a huge impact on the faith of their kids. That statement alone has huge implications for the church and how we do youth ministry. If parents have that heavy of an influence on their teenagers' lives, and we want to disciple teenagers to have a lasting faith, then the church has got to begin to partner with families.

This shouldn't be new knowledge to us. From the beginning, God was intentional in reminding us just how important it is for the family to be the basis of basic discipleship. We read this mandate in Deuteronomy 6:4-9 where it says, "Hear, O Israel: The Lord our God, the Lord is one. Love the Lord your God with all of your heart and with all of your soul and with all your strength. These commandments that I give you today are to be on your hearts. Impress them on your children. Talk about them when you sit and when you get up. Tie them as symbols on your hands and bind them on your foreheads. Write them on the doorframe of your houses and on your gates."

God understood that the spiritual stories that would be passed on between families could be one of the most life-giving tools. He also knew that intentionality would be key when it comes to passing on faith from one generation to another. He doesn't only suggest that we be intentional either. He commands families to be intentional with such urgency because He knows the stakes are high.

I grew up in Upstate New York for the majority of my life in a little town called Plattsburgh. Plattsburgh was the type of place that was great to raise a family but probably not somewhere you would take a vacation. My father was a pastor for over 12 years in that community. We had a decent sized church and a decent sized youth group where I was incredibly active and which had a huge impact on my own call to ministry. We had an awesome youth pastor whom I loved and respected, and to this day is still one of the biggest influences in my life. However, we noticed something different about the families in our church. It wasn't their connection to my dad or to the youth pastor. What we noticed was that they were intentional about spiritual formation in their homes.

Intentionality meant that they spent time with other families in their community who shared the same values. It meant that they made it a priority to read Scripture and pray together with their families in their homes. These families weren't afraid to live counterculturally and to choose to stand up for what they believed was right. Parents would tell their kids stories of God's faithfulness as well as talk about the places where He was challenging them. They created space in their homes for questions and doubts, brought other adults into their kids' lives whose faith story was contagious, and continued to model what it meant to put Jesus first in all things. Additionally, they were intentional about partnering with the church. As a result, many of their kids, who are now grown adults with families, are serving, ministering, and walking with Jesus today, fully surrendered to His ways.

When Church and Family Unite

While we know statistically that discipleship works best when we partner with the family, as youth pastors, we often push back on it out of fear. We think that if we begin to focus on family ministry, we will lose our youth ministries all together and it will somehow lessen our effectiveness or even our creativity. This belief is further away from the truth than we could imagine. Partnering with the family for holistic discipleship isn't about trading in youth ministry for family ministry. It's about bringing families towards the center of the discipleship process and recognizing that when the church and family partner together, we are just better. The big question is, how do we do that?

Partnering with families for holistic discipleship is more than just getting the right tools into their hands. It involves several key components. First, it requires a *commitment* to bring many other Jesus-loving adults into the picture to help mentor and guide our kids. There's an old saying, "It takes a village to raise a child." The truth is, "It takes about 900 villages to raise a teenager!" In her book *Sticky Faith*, Powell talks about this very thing, referring to it as a 5:1 ratio. For every one teen, we want five adults investing in their life.[4] As a teenager, I had about 5-10 adults who were heavily investing in my life. They weren't just youth pastors or youth leaders either. There were numerous adults in the church who would take me out, mentor me, invite me into conversations, listen, and walk through life with me. Now that I am a youth pastor, I want the same for the teens who walk through the doors of my church. It should be our goal to have at least five Jesus-loving adults outside of our youth ministries investing in our teens, providing solid support for families as they holistically disciple their teenagers.

A second key component to partnering with families is to *equip* them. Many families, while they have the desire to disciple their kids, have absolutely no idea where to start. One of our jobs as leaders is to help provide the best tools and resources possible for our families to thrive. This may look like sharing web resources, book titles, and articles that we as leaders are immersing ourselves in to help navigate teenage **Encouraging parents may be as simple as speaking words of affirmation when you observe their teenager contributing within your youth ministry.** culture and spirituality. It may look like hosting a parenting seminar which can provide more in depth training on discipling your child. It may even be as simple as gathering parents together and sharing your thoughts on the latest trends, news, music, or cultural norms our teens are navigating.

A third key component to partnering with families is to *communicate* with them. In a day where calendars are full, families are running tirelessly from event to event, and the demands are never ending, communication is key in partnering. Most parents love when we do everything in our power to over-communicate to make sure they know what is going on. Whether it's a printable calendar, a church website, a weekly parent email, flyers, text messaging, or taking advantage of the social media world, the more we can communicate dates, times, expectations, and more, the better. Communicating with parents reminds them that you understand the stresses put on their life and you want to do everything you can to come alongside them.

A fourth key component to partnering with families is to *challenge* them. A few months back, I challenged my youth group to read through the book of Psalms. We had been talking about the importance of Scripture and I shared with them a Bible app they could access on their phones that would make it easy to read a Psalm a day. I made it a point to include this challenge in our parent email, encouraging parents to accept the challenge with their teens. Within a few days, I watched as parents became excited about reading

Scripture with their teens on the way to school and were even posting key verses that had spoken to their family via social media. Again, it's not that parents don't want to disciple their kids, but sometimes they need a place to start and a person to hold them accountable. "Challenging" may be giving them a weekly task to do as a family, providing a list of questions to ask their kids in response to something you have been teaching, or asking them to participate in a 30-day Scripture reading plan. Challenging our families not only holds them accountable to the discipleship process, but it also provides a practical way to begin the discipleship process.

A fifth key component to partnering with families is to *encourage* them. For those of us who are parents, we know that parenting often feels like a no-win battle. There are days where you look at your kid and wonder if anything you are doing makes a difference. Parents are searching for encouragement, and we have this incredible opportunity to be the encouragers. Encouraging parents may be as simple as speaking words of affirmation when you observe their teenager contributing within your youth ministry. It may be celebrating milestones with families such as birthdays, getting a license, getting into colleges, getting baptized, and making significant spiritual decisions. Encouraging parents may be as simple as inviting them out for lunch to share all the awesome things you love about their teenager, or giving them a small gift to encourage them to do something for themselves.

Another way to encourage is by strategically getting families together in the same place. Most parents are looking for affirmation that they are not alone in the challenges they are facing in parenting a teenager. If we can create spaces where parents begin to have conversations with each other about some of the challenges they face, their shared stories will create a sense of encouragement. This may be as simple as inviting two families over for dinner, creating an open forum, or simply introducing families to one another.

Finally, a sixth component to partnering with families is to *disciple* the parents. Churches often specialize in youth and children's ministries but struggle to focus on and develop parents, who we know are the greatest contributors to passing on faith to the next generation. The pastor of a church in our area invests weekly in a group of men because he believes that if he can develop them spiritually, it will have an impact on the entire family.

Dealing with Dysfunctional Families

I first met Brandon in the church parking lot, where he and his friends had been skateboarding (which happened to be adjacent to my house). Brandon had long hair, black mascara, black nail polish, and was dressed completely in black. My husband and I decided to introduce ourselves to Brandon and his friends and later that night invited them to a youth event we were hosting. Surprisingly, they showed up. That night began this incredible journey of teaching both our teens and our adults how to embrace people outside the walls of our church. It also challenged the way we thought about coming alongside teens whose families are dysfunctional.

It didn't take long to discover that Brandon, and the 10-15 friends he would wind up bringing, all came from very broken home situations. Brandon in particular lived in a small one-room apartment with his mother, who was doing everything to try to make ends meet but was making quite a few poor decisions along the way. Within a few months, Brandon introduced us to his mom, but beyond introductions, we didn't have a whole lot of contact with her. When we did see her, she would remind us of how grateful she was for her son to have us in his life, but that was about it.

Our challenge is to create a healthy culture, not only within our youth group, but within the families themselves. Sometimes when we look at the families that our teens come from, it can feel like we are in a losing battle. When we know that parents are at the top of the list for having the most influence, and then we see a parent who is disinterested in faith, it can be discouraging. For many of us, if we were to do a cross section of our youth ministries, it is likely that we would find that more and more teens come from non-traditional homes. Many are living with grandparents, aunts, uncles, or single parents. Within the home, we see more substance abuse, mental health issues, and just overall messiness. Homes can be really difficult places for our teens to function in, let alone grow spiritually. What do we do with that?

Actually, there are several things we can do. The first is simply to begin by entering their story. Sometimes we think that by inviting a person to church, they will just automatically say yes and life will change for them. For Brandon and his mom, church was never a priority and faith was never really talked about, so coming to church wasn't really on the radar. While Brandon would attend youth group, he wouldn't come Sunday mornings and his mom wouldn't step foot in the church at all — so we decided to do everything we could to enter their story. We would pick Brandon up for youth group, drop him off, and often have conversations about faith, doubts, and everyday life. We had some of the most honest conversations in that church van that I believe led to a deepening of his faith.

As he shared stories about his mom, whom he loved dearly, we would listen and pray together. When we found out where she worked, which happened to be at our favorite coffee joint, we would drop in and just tell her how much we loved spending time with her son. There were times we dropped off gift cards when they were struggling, bought skateboards to find common ground, and stayed up until the late hours of the night to make sure he knew we were there for him.

When it comes to teenagers, our churches have this incredible opportunity to be an adoptive family to them, and for a teenager coming from a difficult home situation, this can make a profound difference.

We were not the only ones doing those things. Brandon, without even knowing it, had created this culture of welcome that had shifted our entire youth ministry's focus in an awesome way. As we shared his story to the church board, our ministry leaders, and our pastoral staff, they also began to invest in his life by getting to know him, praying for him, and showing up where they could. These adults wound up being mentors in Brandon's life, creating an almost surrogate family system for him.

When it comes to teenagers, our churches have this incredible opportunity to be an adoptive family to them, and for a teenager coming from a difficult home situation, this can make a profound difference. We do this by *showing up for the big things*. I remember one of our teens asking my husband and I to walk with him for his senior night during his lacrosse season because he felt as though we had been family to him. Showing up may be as simple as that. We show up for the big things by attending graduations, visiting workplaces on the first day, and attending games and concerts our teens have worked hard to be part of. Showing up for the big things also includes attending funerals, court dates, and just being there for our teens when they've received disappointing news.

We can be an adoptive family to our teens by *providing accountability and prayer*. We can ask the hard questions, do a lot of listening, challenge them to think about what they believe, and create spaces for these things to happen. We can find committed people in the church who are willing to pray for not only our teens but their families, by name, for the specific needs and challenges they are dealing with.

When a church makes the commitment to operate as an adoptive family for our teenagers, it's a commitment to be intentional. It starts with being intentional about *being accepting*. Our job as the church isn't to change our teens or their families. Our job is to invite them into a community where they can experience the love of God that ultimately brings about change. When we can embrace our teens and their families just as they are, despite how messy it gets, we create a culture of welcome, and that culture is transformational. We love each other through the mess of middle and high school and then love them beyond that. When we can make a commitment to love our teens post-high school, walking with them as they make decisions in college and beyond, we send a signal that they are truly a part of our family, and this has the potential to change everything.

There were a few times when I wanted to give up on Brandon, but we as a church had made the commitment that we were going to love him regardless of his decisions. I kept telling Brandon that one day he would make a decision for Jesus, so just wait. When he graduated he moved away and he still had not made that decision.

Several years later, my phone rang. On the other end was a familiar voice. "Pastor Andrea? I just wanted you to know I did what you said I would always do one day. I gave my life to Jesus." I think I dropped the phone and then started sobbing. The investment, despite the messiness, had paid off. Several months later he came home and we baptized him, with a whole lot of the church present. Standing next to the baptismal was his mom. That day was a reminder of why the hard work of youth ministry and patient discipleship is worth it.

We never know how much influence we will have on a teenager or their family, but our job as the church is to do everything in our power to come alongside our teens and their families. We aren't responsible for the results, but we are responsible for staying committed to the mission of reaching people for Jesus. For Sarah, the young lady from my volleyball team, she never came to Christ, but our connection to her led to a connection to her older sister, who eventually gave her life to Christ, along with her fiancé. They are now married and serving in the church. We're still praying that the seeds that were planted, the mentorships that were forged, the showing up that played out … somehow that will lead her to a decision for Jesus one day, just like it did for Brandon.

Start Small and Start Somewhere

Whether you find yourself working with amazing, functional, Jesus-loving families or you are in the midst of some really messy and broken systems, your job is the same. Help teens fall in love with Jesus in a way that changes everything. The best possible way to do that is to work alongside their families, whether that be the biological family or the adoptive family. You'll be tempted to think you have to have a massive plan in place to begin, but my encouragement is to start small and start somewhere. You never know who you might reach.

Bonus: 16 Creative Ideas to Get Started

Not sure where to get started??? Here are a few ideas for you.

1. *Parent Weekly Email:* At the start of each week, send out an email with upcoming events and details, payments that are due, helpful articles about youth culture and parenting, and topics you are preaching/teaching on. Feel free to add a few sentences as to how God has been moving in your youth group and let parents know you are praying for them.

2. *Parent Newsletter:* Send out a monthly newsletter that includes helpful articles on parenting, youth cultural trends, highlights from the youth ministry, etc. For a great newsletter that is already done for you, and doesn't cost a lot to purchase, visit www.cpyu.org.

3. *Family Training Weekend:* Invite a trained professional in youth ministry to come in and do a weekend parenting seminar. If finances are an issue, partner with another local church to split the cost, or invite a local youth pastor who has been in youth ministry for a long time to come and share. You could also include mental health care providers, counselors, and even older adults who have parented teens before to be a part of the weekend.

4. *Family Creative Prayer Stations:* Host a night of prayer where families can come together and engage in creative prayer stations (prayer station ideas can be found online). Provide clear instructions as to what families are to do at each station. At the end, provide some of those ideas on paper for families to take and implement at their own homes.

5. **Back to School Family Prayer:** Invite families to sign up for 15-minute blocks of time to meet with you at the start of the school year and pray for them. Ask them what they are celebrating from the summer and what challenges you can pray for at the beginning of the school year.

6. **Parent Connection:** Provide a monthly gathering where you briefly share a topic or issue pertaining to youth and/or parenting, and then provide discussion questions for table groups to talk through.

7. **Dinner Nights:** Before major mid-week programming, have a dinner available for families to participate in. Ask older families in the church to help cook simple dinners (like spaghetti, tacos, hot dogs, etc.), and then charge a small fee for each family to participate. If you can get donations, make it free!

8. **Parallel Teaching:** Work with your lead pastor and try to teach on the same Scripture passages or series. This helps create a sense of continuity for the family and provides talking points as well.

9. **Sticky Faith Curriculum:** Check out the website www.stickyfaith.org for some great parent and teen curriculum. Host a parent Sunday School class and work through the Sticky Faith curriculum together.

10. **Debrief Major Events:** As soon as you come back from an event like teen camp, retreat, mission trip, etc., ask parents to stay for an extra 30 minutes when they come to pick up their teens. Spend that 30 minutes recapping the event, sharing highlights, and offering challenges. Give a sheet of questions that parents can ask their kids as they head home.

11. **Let Parents Be Storytellers:** Invite parents of your teenagers to come to youth group and share their story of how they came to know Christ. You could also have a panel of parents come and ask them questions about their faith stories at youth group.

12. **Invite Families Into Your Home:** The best way to get to know families is by eating together! Invite a couple of families over for lunch or dinner at the same time. This gives you a chance to get to know the families and also gives the families ways to connect with each other.

13. **Family Missions/Serve Days:** Find ways to serve together. Whether it's a weeklong intergenerational missions trip or an afternoon of serving at

a local compassionate ministry, serving together creates some incredible discipleship opportunities.

14. **Encouraging Notes:** Send mail! A handwritten note of encouragement can go a long way and help families to feel known, seen, and that they are not alone.

15. **Mentorship/Prayer Partner Plan:** Create prayer profiles for all of the teens in your ministry and ask for people in your congregation to adopt a prayer partner. Kick this ministry off with a prayer breakfast where teens and adults can meet each other face to face and commit to praying for one another for a year.

16. **Parenting Partners:** Match moms and dads up with other adults who have parented well in the past and are in the next stage of life. These "match ups" can serve as prayer partners, discipleship mentors, and encouragers for the journey.

CHAPTER 6

Relational Discipleship:
Viewing Our Life As Our Curriculum

Bakhoh Jatmiko

Bakhoh Jatmiko is the Sealands Field Youth Coordinator and pastor who serves in Yogyakarta, Indonesia. Youth ministry is exciting to him because there is a new generation with passion for the Lord. Discipleship is important to Bakhoh because Christlikeness does not appear suddenly in a single moment or as the result of a single experience. Discipleship helps the believer to walk on a spiritual journey to be more Christlike.

Our need for relationship is highlighted at the very beginning of our story. In Genesis, God declares, "It's not good that the human is alone" (Genesis 2:18, CEB). God knew we were created to be in relationship with each other and with God. Throughout the rest of Scripture, we see the significance of relationship. While relationships are hard and challenging, the stories of trust, support, friendship, and love are also the stories of survival, perseverance, joy, and hope. We need each other as we journey through life. I believe that when God says that it is not good for humans to be alone, He was not talking about increasing how many followers we have on social media. I believe God wants us to have genuine relationships where life is shared.

In this chapter, we are going to explore how, if we are intentional, our everyday lives can serve as our greatest discipleship resource for our youth. Using this "built-in" longing for connection and relationships, we can set the stage for meaningful discipleship to occur.

> **Jesus used His life as a living curriculum, and the foundation for this was His relationship with the disciples.**

When we look at Jesus' ministry, we see a very clear pattern of Him putting relationships as the foundation of His ministry. Jesus called each of His disciples with a personal calling, "Come and follow me." Then, for three and a half years Jesus walked, talked, ministered, laughed, cried, and journeyed with these twelve men. He didn't get their commitment card and then check in with them from time to time. These relationships were ongoing and real. The disciples were called, not only to listen to Jesus' teaching or do His commands, but to follow Jesus closely and to really connect with Him.

In the ministry context, we have to always beware of superficial relationships or the *pseudo-relationship* trap. The pseudo-relationship is formed when we begin focusing on activities or programs rather than real relationships. Activities and programs can be a way to draw people in, but they do not give us a guarantee of anything more. Developing these meaningful relationships matters because discipleship demands intentionality and relationship. Relationship is a way of connecting others to Jesus through our lives. As we faithfully live out our faith before others, we embody for them the teachings and words of Jesus. Our lives are constantly pointing back to Jesus, because the goal is not to make followers for ourselves but disciples of Jesus.

Life as Our Curriculum

Curriculum is simply a set of lessons or classes used to help a student master a given subject. In church, we often think of our Sunday School materials or small group lesson guides as curriculum. These resources help give a focus to what we teach our youth.

When I read and study the Bible, I find it fascinating to study how Jesus did discipleship, how He taught His disciples. There were no lessons or printed study guides. Jesus taught often, but these teaching times are generally lessons in response to something that has happened rather than the carrying out of a scheduled lecture. As I read the Bible, what I see is mostly Jesus letting His disciples watch what He did, observe how He dealt with the marginalised, and pay attention to how He treated the weak. In short, Jesus wanted them to really experience His way of living life. Jesus gave them opportunities to encounter the ups and downs of life along with Him and learn. Jesus used His life as a living curriculum, and the foundation for this was His relationship with the disciples. "Without relationship, there is no discipleship, just the passing of information."[1] Thus, Jesus not only gave the disciples knowledge by lecturing to them, but He transformed His disciples lives through living life together with them.

If we accept the invitation to open our lives up to our youth as a means of discipling them, we must live our lives genuinely and with an awareness of the example we are setting for them.

From Jesus, we know that discipleship is not only about remembering truths taught and being able to repeat them. Discipleship goes beyond that. Of course I believe programs, curricula, and materials are important in the discipleship process, however, putting those truths into practice is the key. The Greek word for learner, *mathētes*, which is the root of our word mathematics, means "thought accompanied by endeavour."[2] Learning must involve doing. Disciples think and learn, but if they are truly learning the lessons of their teacher, they must move beyond listening and thinking to doing. This can begin by choosing to act in the way the one they follow acts.

I can look back at my own life and notice how seeing the way others lived served as a discipleship opportunity for me and caused me to grow in how I lived out my faith. I thought I understood love fairly well, but I learned even more about love when I saw my friend Mery visit an old, sick, poor, and lonely widow to bring her meals, clean her up, and change her smelly and dirty clothes. I thought I understood the meaning of sacrifice fairly well, but I learned even more when I discovered that Edward, a university student, gave his end-of-month money to one of our church members who needed money to buy a book for her son.

If we accept the invitation to open our lives up to our youth as a means of discipling them, we must live our lives genuinely and with an awareness of the example we are setting for them. The reality is that we serve as examples to them whether we are thinking about it or not. So, if Christ is in us, His love and His life must be reflected through our life. Let us live in such a way that we may proclaim along with Paul, "Follow my example, as I follow the example of Christ" (1 Corinthians 11:1).

So, what will this look like? Do we just walk around with our youth group following behind us all day? I want to suggest three examples of how we can position our lives to serve as a living curriculum.

Doing Activities Together

As we discussed earlier, Jesus did not have a set time for daily lectures or a specific location. Instead, bravely I would say, Jesus taught His disciples without any apparent schedules or programs. Jesus engaged His disciples in doing life together and His times of teaching typically followed or preceded an activity where the lesson had been modelled or practiced.

When Jesus wanted the disciples to learn about His authority over creation, He brought them out on a lake and experienced with them the storm and the waves tossing the boat. When He wanted the disciples to learn about trusting God to be their provider, He led them to the needy and collaborated with them to supply all the people's needs. When Jesus wanted the disciples to learn what it means to follow the God of life, He led them to Lazarus' tomb, where he had laid for four days and called Lazarus back to life.

By walking together with Jesus, the disciples could see His reaction when He was touched by the unclean woman. The disciples learned what it meant to show perfect love when Jesus reached out and touched the leper who came to Him. Jesus let the disciples hear the Pharisees and Sadducees criticize Him and try to trap Him and learn what it meant to respond with divine wisdom.

Most of Jesus' teachings were not presented lectures, rather He artfully wove His teaching into the events of daily life. His teaching flowed out of His relationship with His companions and the crowds who followed Him. He used every opportunity to transform their ways of thinking and their lives. When Jesus called His disciples to follow Him, He made His life their curriculum.

My friend Ishak is one of the many people who have helped me become more like Christ. Ishak and I have a common interest: climbing mountains. We have had lots of adventures together while mountain climbing, and he has taught me many meaningful lessons during those climbs.

One day during a climb, we reached a slippery, narrow slope upward where the path got up to a 50-degree incline on our way to the peak. This track made me exhausted. I was tempted to quit and go back home. I started to grumble and ask myself why I had even decided to climb that mountain in the first place. I was very surprised when I heard Ishak's response to our tiring situation. He said, "Our life is just like this. Sometimes God lets you walk in a high, narrow and rocky slope of life, but you have to believe that He also promises to bring you to the green valley. What you need to do is give thanks in every situation." What? Here I was hardly able to breath, and Ishak comes up with a spiritual lesson and explained it all to me! He was right … he was also in better shape than me!

His short statement hit right on the target. I was struck by the Holy Spirit and convicted about my irritability. That one small explanation by Ishak changed my view about life. Although it happened nearly 15 years ago, I can still picture it as if it were today. It is stuck deep in my heart. For me, that was the most powerful preaching ever prepared by a preacher.

As we begin discipling in this way, we will need to be very mindful of when these teaching moments arise. We need to be in prayer and ask the Holy Spirit to guide us and help us know what lessons our youth need. It will also be essential for us to spend time with our youth outside of church. Organize sports activities and watch for opportunities to share about fairness, working together towards a common goal or conclusion. Go for walks around your city and identify ways to help those in need. Challenge your youth to consider the dignity of these individuals and how our help should always be respectful. Invite them to help with planning an event. You'll be able to talk about everything from stewardship to ethical business practices to serving others. We can plan times to go camping, hiking, swimming, or fishing. We can cook, watch a movie, or form a book club. There are so many possibilities. The key lesson is simply that doing activities together is a great way to create space for discipleship.

Modelling in Cheers and Tears

Through the discipleship process of youth, it is important for us to be a model of an authentic and faithful Jesus-follower. Our youth are watching us to see how we respond to whatever life brings our way — both the good and bad. How we respond to the crises of life is a critical moment in teaching how Jesus' disciples live. Do we try to solve every crisis in our own strength? Do we prayerfully seek God's guidance in order to make strong and wise choices? Do we justify bad short cuts in order to simplify our life? How we react to crises says more about in whom or in what we put our trust than whatever words we say.

Crisis moments serve as genuine reflections of what guides our lives. Sharing our life as a curriculum means that we have to be ready to let our youth see and learn from us both in our cheers and our tears. It is natural for us to resist inviting people into the difficult times in our lives, and there are healthy boundaries to respect. However, if our youth know that we are going through a hard time, we shouldn't act like it doesn't exist when we are around them. They need to see us both wrestle with and trust God during those times. In the book *Real-Life Discipleship Training Manual: Equipping Disciples Who Make Disciples* it says,

> "Without relationship between believers, there is no model to follow, no authenticity, no accountability, no application, and no support for the journey. These things come through personal contacts. And because that relational context for learning is lacking, life change is much rarer than it should be among Christians today."[3]

Sometimes life is like a calm, flowery garden, but not usually. In real life we laugh and cry, celebrate and mourn. Our response to these extremes reveals our loyalty, faith, and integrity. A life well lived serves as a model for others and creates an environment where others are able to grow as well. In such an environment, we become effective disciple-makers even in our tears.

I had only been married to Ester, my wife, for a happy and sweet three years of marriage when our life came to a halt with some heart-breaking news. Several months prior, my wife had been stricken by severe pain in her abdomen. We decided to see a doctor to try and understand what was happening. After the doctor examined her, she found a large cyst on my wife's right ovary. We were shocked, especially Ester, because just four years earlier she had already undergone an operation for removing a large cyst on her left ovary. That time was incredibly difficult for us, probably the most difficult time of our marriage so far. The doctor said it was possible my wife would need to have another operation and warned us that afterwards we might not be able to have children.

Some of the youth in our church knew what we were going through. They were watching and paying attention to see how we would respond to this crisis. They knew the "real me" would show through. Would I show my frustration and disappointment with cursing or complaining, blaming myself or others, or God? Would I ask where God's promised protections were? Would I question God because He let us go through this? Or would I choose the opposite reactions and keep believing and trusting God's plan?

I thank God for helping me live out my faith well even in the midst of such a difficult situation. I kept praying and striving to demonstrate the faith I often preached about in my sermons and in our discipleship meetings. That was a perfect moment for my youth to learn from the "living curriculum" of my life. Several weeks after my wife was diagnosed with the cyst, we went back to the doctor to learn about the progress. When the doctor started to examine my wife with the ultrasound machine, she said that there was nothing; she could not find any cyst! We praise Jesus! He answered our prayer and as I write this chapter, we just celebrated the first birthday of our beautiful baby daughter.

By watching me and learning from my "living curriculum," the youth learned that this Jesus who lived 2,000 years ago also lives today and is actively at work in our world. They learned about Jesus' authority, not only by what I said, but by what they saw demonstrated in our family. They learned what life looks like when our faith truly impacts our day-to-day lives. Most importantly, they are growing in faith and in their commitment to follow Jesus as His disciples.

Sharing Our Personal Space

It is not always easy to let others cross into our personal space. Usually we tightly guard against letting very many people into the more personal areas of our life. We often have some kind of requirements for letting people in. They are either family or we have a shared connection where we've come to trust them. However, to make our life a living curriculum means we have to let others see and enter into some of those areas we'd rather protect. Again, this isn't a call to tear down all boundaries. Boundaries are helpful and healthy and safe. It is, however, a call to examine how often we keep our relationships at a superficial level and in turn sacrifice any influence their lives. We cannot influence the people we disciple if we keep them at a distance. Sharing life means to invite them to come closer and have deeper conversations, ask harder questions, and form more trusting relationships. Discipleship requires meaningful conversation, not just small talk; sincere attention, not just sugar coating; and intense coaching, not just brief check-in meetings.

Jesus himself let His disciples cross the line and enter His personal space. I believe it was not easy for Jesus to accept all of their various different backgrounds either. But the problem actually went both ways! As they came into deeper relationship with Jesus, it meant Jesus would enter more fully into their lives as well. Once they became Jesus' disciples, it also meant they were living life with the other disciples. I can't imagine this was easy for them. The twelve disciples, as a group, were in no way "natural" friends. It is difficult to think of positions and perspectives more opposite than that of a tax collector and a zealot. And yet their being gathered together presupposed a certain common purpose that required walking together, eating together, living together, and getting to know each other well.

We cannot influence the people we disciple if we keep them at a distance.

Even though it is not easy to let others cross into our personal space, in the discipleship process it is not an option but a requirement in helping others grow. Mother Mary Francis writes:

"If we do not call each other friends, then let us not pretend that we can call each other sisters. We cannot have real sisters who are not real friends. And so it goes with every human relationship."[4]

We must form friendships with our brothers and sisters in Christ whom we are discipling. This will often mean letting our cosy personal zones be interrupted by others. They will likely have different backgrounds. For our youth, they will often have different world views, but we are all on the journey of becoming more like Christ, and we need to walk with each other through our ups and downs. As authentic disciples, we need to build loving relationships within the body of Christ and express that love through a willingness to deny self-interest in deference to the needs of fellow disciples. This is the "same love" Paul describes in Philippians 2:1-11, where he exhorts the disciples to imitate the self-sacrificing attitude of Christ in their relationships with one another.

One way to invite people to enter into our personal space is to invite them to come to our house or place where we stay. We may invite them to have some tea or coffee in our backyard, cook together in our kitchen, have lunch or dinner with them, let them sit on our sofa or lay back in our rocking chair. This might all take place prior to a more formal time of discipleship where we study the Bible, pray, or work through our discipleship agenda. However, by inviting them into our home, it means that we let them see how we arrange our room and how we live. They will see what is on our bookshelf and know what kinds of books we read. They will see our DVD collection and know what kind of movies we watch. They will hear our playlist and know what kind of music we listen to. They will notice how we treat our family members and will know how we demonstrate our love. In other words, by inviting them to see where we spend the majority of our time, we will let them see our world, our genuine habits and attitudes, and our quality of life.

Based on my personal experience, this will become an effective and important stage in building relationships with the people you disciple. They will feel accepted and important. Accepting them as friends is the most basic reason outsiders come into Christian churches and communities.[5] When they feel genuine friendship, they will be connected with us, and that is where trust can be built. And when trust is built, they will open their lives to us and we can share the values and teachings the Lord is guiding us to share.

The Value of Comfortable and Safe Spaces

It should go without saying, but throughout these efforts to build relationships as a foundation for discipleship, it is important to note that everything must be done in places and ways that are comfortable and safe for our youth. We must be careful to never put additional burdens on them or force them to do something that they do not want to do. The goal is discipleship. Jesus said, "Come to me, all you who are weary and burdened, and I will give you rest. Take my yoke upon you and learn from me, for I am gentle and humble in heart, and you will find rest for your souls. For my yoke is easy and my burden is light" (Matthew 11:28-30). Our youth carry many burdens and many fears. We need to be sensitive to their needs and meet them where they are. Our youth are learning what it means to follow Jesus, and they won't do it perfectly all the time. Part of what we should be modelling in our living curriculum is the unconditional and perfect love of God. If we can model this well, then we will be laying a strong foundation for our relational discipleship with our youth.

Additionally, providing comfortable and safe spaces for our youth means that they have a place where they are seen and heard. Our youth are more connected than ever on social media and online, and yet youth today report feeling incredibly lonely and isolated. They need safe spaces where they can be themselves, where they can share their ideas and their fears, and where they are loved and accepted for who they are. Jesus loved people this way and this lesson must be a central part of our living curriculum.

> Our youth are learning what it means to follow Jesus, and they won't do it perfectly all the time. Part of what we should be modelling in our living curriculum is the unconditional and perfect love of God.

This doesn't mean God will never ask us to share a word of challenge with our youth. Jesus had hard words for His disciples from time to time. However, if we have built a strong relationship and there is trust and unconditional love, then it is more likely our youth will be able to hear us saying those challenging words in love.

Relationships are complicated. Keeping discipleship to a Wednesday night program with a printed curriculum is much easier and safer. However, discipleship doesn't truly take root until God's word moves from our head to our heart and out through our hands and feet. Discipleship is not about the four walls of a classroom. Discipleship is about sharing with others our lives and experiences as we walk together in our journey with Jesus.

WORKS CITED/NOTES

Introduction

1. Sweet, Leonard. *Nudge: Awakening Each Other to the God Who's Already There*. David C. Cook, 2010.
2. Yaconelli, Mark. *Contemplative Youth Ministry: Practicing the Presence of Jesus*. Zondervan/ Youth Specialties, 2006.
3. Gunter, W. Stephen, Scott J. Jones, Ted A. Campbell, Rebekah L. Miles, Randy L. Maddox. *Wesley and the Quadrilateral: Renewing the Conversation*. Abingdon Press, 1997.

Chapter 1

1. Leys, Lucas. *El Ministerio Juvenil Efectivo*. Editorial Vida, 2003.
2. Ibid.
3. Ortíz, Félix, Annette Gulick, Gerardo Muniello. *Raíces: Pastoral juvenil en profundidad*. Editorial Vida, 2008.
4. Leys, Lucas. *El Ministerio Juvenil Efectivo*. Editorial Vida, 2003.
5. Maxwell, John C. *The 21 Irrefutable Laws of Leadership [Las 21 leyes irrefutables del liderazgo]*. Thomas Nelson, Inc., 1998.
6. Ibid.

Chapter 3

1. Nouwen, Henri J. M., Michael J. Christensen, Rebecca J. Laird. *Spiritual Formation: Following the Movements of the Spirit [Formación Espiritual: Siguiendo los Impulsos del Espíritu]*. Sal Terrae, 2011.
2. Foster, Richard J. *Celebration of Discipline [Alabanza a la Disciplina]*. Editorial Betania, 1986.
3. Wesley, Juan. *Sermones de Juan Wesley: Tomo I*. Nazarene Publishing House, 1990.
4. Tracy, Wesley D., E. Dee Freeborn, Janine Tartaglia, Morris A. Weigelt. *Formación Espiritual*. Casa Nazarena de Publicaciones, 1999.
5. Foster, Richard J. *Celebration of Discipline [Alabanza a la Disciplina]*. Editorial Betania, 1986.

Chapter 5

1. Powell, Kara E., Chap Clark. *Sticky Faith: Everyday Ideas to Build Lasting Faith in Your Kids*. Zondervan, 2011.
2. Dean, Kenda Creasy. *Almost Christian: What the Faith of Our Teenagers Is Telling the American Church*. Oxford University Press, 2010.
3. Powell, Kara E., Chap Clark. *Sticky Faith: Everyday Ideas to Build Lasting Faith in Your Kids*. Zondervan, 2011.
4. Ibid.

Chapter 6

1. Harrington, Bobby. "Relationships." *Discipleship.org*, discipleship.org/relationships.
2. Newton, Gary C. *Growing Toward Spiritual Maturity*. Evangelical Training Association, 1999.
3. Putman, Jim, Avery T. Willis Jr., Brandon Guindon, Bill Krause. *Real-Life Discipleship Training Manual: Equipping Disciples Who Make Disciples*. NavPress, 2010.
4. Francis, Mother Mary. *But I Have Called You Friends: Reflections on the Art of Christian Friendship*. Ignatius Press, 2006.
5. Kreider, Alan, Eleanor Kreider. *Worship & Mission after Christendom*. Herald Press, 2011.

www.ingramcontent.com/pod-product-compliance
Lightning Source LLC
Chambersburg PA
CBHW021140020426
42331CB00005B/843